ONE MILLION FROGS

ONE MILLION FROGS

LESSONS ABOUT ENTREPRENEURSHIP LEARNED THE HARD WAY

PETER GASCA | RHETT POWER

MILL CITY PRESS
MINNEAPOLIS, MN

Mill City Press, Inc.
322 First Avenue N, 5th floor
Minneapolis, MN 55401
612.455.2293
www.millcitypublishing.com

For information about special discounts for bulk purchases, please contact
info@onemillionfrogs.com

To book the authors for speaking or other guest appearances,
Contact
booking@rhettpower.com
booking@petergasca.com

ISBN-13: 978-1-63413-907-6
LCCN: 2016906219

Book Design by B. Cook

Illustrations by Robert Hawkins

www.onemillionfrogs.com
www.rhettpower.com
www.petergasca.com

Printed in the United States of America

DEDICATIONS - AUTHORS

I would like to dedicate this book to my dad, whose moral and financial support is what made my entrepreneurial journey possible. He is the ultimate role model of an entrepreneur, a dad, and a person. I love you, Pappy!

-- Peter Gasca

This is for my family, Julie McKay, Max, and Riley. Thanks for the support and sacrifice you made while I was trying to build a business. You gave me the freedom to pursue a dream!

-- Rhett Power

DEDICATIONS - KICKSTARTER PREMIUM CAMPAIGN BACKERS

To Randy White of Kingman, Arizona, my brother and best friend; and to his pal Rocco and his Baby, whom he loves dearly and who gave him purpose and direction.

-- Robert B. White

In loving memory of Arnold Lewis Cohen DPM, who has inspired his children David, Barry and Susan to pursue their entrepreneurial dreams. His inspiration lives on in his grandchildren Sara, Nika, Noah, Kira and Ava. May they too find their entrepreneurial wings and reinvent the world!

-- Barry Cohen

In memory of Amelia and Enrique Sandan, whose perseverance and hard work I have strived to emulate. You rarely complained about life, blamed other people, or worried about the little things. You always demanded perfection, even though you knew inside it wasn't always possible. They say there's a difference between being wealthy in life and being rich in life, and without a doubt, you were the richest people I've ever known.

-- Erwin Sandan

To my grandfathers, Glenn Shoaf and Leonard Moretz, whose hard work and commitment to building their businesses and community set an example for me and helped to provide opportunities for many others.

-- Ashley Moretz

To my grandfather, a man that grew up with so little and so lonely, but overcame the obstacles to build a family, used the energy of his youth to build them a home, created a business in his basement and never stopped learning. It was hearing him speak English when I was a child that made me want to learn the language; once I did, a whole new world opened up to me and now I live in it. Thank you.

-- Margarita Muzzall

To my hubby Brian, who is my rock, and who is also taking his first small step to being entrepreneur!

-- May Chan

To Dr. David McNaul, a man of honor, courage, and compassion that never gave up on his dream. A man who has sacrificed for his country and demonstrates his commitment to helping others daily. A true inspiration.

-- Vicki McNaul

CONTENTS

ACKNOWLEDGMENTS

We would like to thank the following people for their generous contributions to our Kickstarter campaign. Thank you for making this book possible!

A.J. Rea
Adam Sharp
Ainel Alberth
Alberto Abadia
American Ninth Art Studios, LLC
Ami Arqui-Edwards
Andres Riggioni
Annalisa Lolli
Barbara B
Barbara Wagner
Barry Cohen
Bernard Nossuli
Beth Flores
Bill Hinson
Bobbe Barnes
Bryan Knowlton
Corinna Milliken
Caesar Layton
Christopher Stitt
Corrine Gonos
Daniel O'Connor
David Benedick
David Ford
David Gasca
David Rice
Devon George
Dollie Silpasuvan
Donald Power
Dr. David Powers
Eileen Song Kim
Emily Johnson
Erin Suzanne Johnson
Erwin Sandan
Evangelina Sundgrenz
Eve Rebennack
George Ashley Moretz
Jason Burak
Jeanette Powell
Jesse Mejia
Jill McGlaughlin
Jill Rea

Jocelyn Flint
Judi Heichelheim
Justin Jarman
Karolina Jaskola
Leah Hoffman
Linda Russell
Linda Sullivan
Lisa Grouette
M.C.A. Hogarth
Margarita Muzzall
Mark Kukla
May Chan
Meredith Bell
Michael Lolli
Michelle Ford
Michelle Thomas
Mike Schroll
Mito Tsukumoto
Nicolette Green
Paul Reynolds
Peter Gasca Sr.
Richelle Pillard
Robert Hawkins
Ron Ferry
Ronny Engelke
Samuel Leavitt
Sara Cochran
Scott Janowski
Scott Nielson
Shannon Mulnix
Sherry Cox
Steve Roth
Steven Spiegel
Tanja
Tatyana Shestopalova
Tiffany Orvet
Tim Blue
Tom Grossman
Tori Gasca
Tracy Hotaling
Travis Poe
Vicki Johnson
Virginia Hutcheon
Zenobia Mertel

INTRODUCTION

The way to get started is to quit talking and start doing.

-- Walt Disney, Co-Founder, Disney

Our entrepreneurial story plays out the way most do: an idea conceived over watered-down Russian beer and flatbread pizza at a quaint Georgian restaurant high in the cool mountains of Kazakhstan.

It pinnacled with the company we founded, Wild Creations, being recognized as one of *Inc. Magazine's* 500 fastest growing private businesses in the US and the number one fastest growing business in South Carolina.

The root of our success: frogs.

We'd like to say that it all went as planned. Nothing, however, went as planned. For starters, our original vision of running a large multinational investment holdings company turned into wrangling frogs and making toys. The transition, of course, was an interesting one and most certainly did not happen overnight.

Along the way, there was more pizza and probably too much beer, mortars in Afghanistan, more miles than most people drive in five lifetimes, cheap hotels with fleas, pilfered toilet paper, extreme government agencies and extremer special interest groups, guns and police, endless trade show pitches and tubes of lip balm, and more than one lonely Christmas season spent at a mall kiosk bartering live frogs.

Okay, so maybe that is not the way most startups go.

It is not, however, as different as you might think. If you replace all of that history with the underlying themes that encouraged them, you will find commonalities. Belt tightening, stress management, risk taking, dedication and long hours, innovative thinking, thriftiness, interpersonal skill development, conflict resolution, hard work, salesmanship, and unending personal sacrifice.

If you ask ten successful entrepreneurs for the secret to success, you will receive twenty unique stories and more than a fair share of clichés. And while most will not involve dodging live ordnance in Afghanistan or frogs, all will share these same themes.

This book is one of those stories.

It's about two regular guys who for years worked in comfortable consulting jobs in "Corporate America," with job security, comfortable paychecks and the freedom to fill numerous passport pages, but who had unfulfilled and conflicting ambitions. It's about our entrepreneurial journey, from our catalysts to taking action through the most significant economic crisis in a generation, and rising from the bowels of complete failure and mediocrity to sitting with John Lasseter, the founder of Pixar, at the Academy Awards of Toys.

All with an improbable frog company.

This book is filled with stories, anecdotes and, yes, a few clichés, but the genesis behind it all was to provide other aspiring entrepreneurs a set of our hard-knock lessons to guide them to their entrepreneurial dreams. Most stories involve mistakes we made along the way that were sometimes avoidable and always expensive. We hope to impart wisdom through what was our collective ignorance.

We understand completely that most aspiring entrepreneurs who read this book will eventually make the same mistakes we have. We are, after all, natural risk takers and universally inquisitive. Entrepreneurs are the type of people who burn themselves on the frying pan because we just had to see "what if." That natural curiosity is what encourages them to venture out and start businesses, build legacies, and leave their marks in this life.

So the greater intent of this book, to a certain extent, is to provide you with validation and inspiration.

The fears and anxieties you have are common. True, some people have more tolerance for risk and, hence, are more inclined to be entrepreneurs, but this book will provide evidence that you don't have to be Elon Musk or Sir Richard Branson to start a business.

All you need is a little common sense, courage, and persistence.

Not necessarily in that order.

And when you fail -- and you will, often -- we hope the stories and anecdotes in this book will serve to provide you with not only the tips to help you be successful, but also the moral support you need to persevere.

You are not alone in your ambition. The first step is the most difficult. Read on and you will come to understand why entrepreneurial success cannot be defined by a single adjective or cliché, but instead only by the embodiment of a complete narrative of another entrepreneur's successes and, more important, perseverance through all the hard times.

CHAPTER ONE

I'm convinced that about half of what separates the successful entrepreneurs from the non-successful ones is pure perseverance.

-- Steve Jobs, Co-Founder and CEO, Apple

SO YOU WANT TO BE AN ENTREPRENEUR?

We should start by explaining how we came to write this book.

We, Pete Gasca and Rhett Power, are the co-founders of Wild Creations, a company best known for its desktop ecosystem habitat with live, aquatic African dwarf frogs. The "EcoAquarium," as we eventually named it, is a small aquarium that sits atop a desk, shelf, or other small space and, because it contains all the biological components necessary to mimic an aquatic ecosystem, requires no filter or chemicals to stay clean.

It's an aquarium you never have to clean. Cool, right?

We loved the idea of the self-cleaning ecosystem habitat -- even formulated our initial company brand after it -- but as much as we loved to talk about how the habitat stayed clean and safe for its inhabitants, consumers loved the frogs.

The frogs were cute, no doubt. At an inch and a half, they lived up (or down) to their official name, "dwarf frogs." They were also completely aquatic, and because they were by nature at the bottom of the food chain, they were passive and thrived in smaller areas. For these reasons, they lived a much longer, healthier and predator-free life in the EcoAquarium.

Though we did not start Wild Creations with a focus on the frogs, we did eventually adopt them as our brand (hence Bob the Frog on our cover) and lead with and eventually become best know for them.

We founded the company in 2007, a year before the collapse of Lehman Brothers rocked the foundation of the US credit market, brought the U.S. economy to its collective knees, and threw the entire globe into the worst economic recession in a generation. Business credit froze completely. People lost their homes in record foreclosures. Cities filed bankruptcy. Television personalities called it an “apocalypse.”

The Great Recession.

It was not, to say the least, a great time to be a small, under-funded retail startup.

Just two short years later, however, in spite of the Great Recession, Wild Creations was recognized by the South Carolina Chamber of Commerce as the number one fastest growing company in the state, and by the *Inc. Magazine* as one of the Top 500 fastest growing company in the U.S. That same year, we were both recognized for our achievements as finalists for the prestigious Ernst and Young *Entrepreneur of the Year Award*.

Needless to say, it did not happen easily, and how two non-science guys with no background in Marine Biology (or any “-ology” for that matter) came to run a complex ecosystem aquarium company will be explained later. First, we would like to address the reason for this book, namely what we believe it takes to be an entrepreneur, and speak directly to those of you who picked up the book hoping to find inspiration.

NATURE VS. NURTURE

When we set out on this entrepreneurial voyage, only Rhett had previously run his own business, a modest kayak rental company in South Carolina. He was in his twenties, and by all comparisons, it was more of a hobby than a business. Regardless, he had undertaken running a business and was familiar, to a certain extent, of what was required. Pete, however, had worked in corporate America his entire life, owning his responsibilities and finding success climbing a couple of corporate ladders. For him, the idea of entrepreneurship had always been an aspiration, but for many of the reasons we will discuss, a pipe dream.

We often debate, over one or a few beers usually, whether someone can be taught to be an entrepreneur or whether it is inherent. Rhett argues that true entrepreneurs are *born* with the characteristics needed to be successful, and through life experiences those characteristics are round out and refined. From the beginning, he epitomized this idea, demonstrating a stoic confidence and the needed perseverance to survive our early (and many) challenges. Pete, on the other hand, believes strongly that one can be *taught* to be an entrepreneur. For him, starting Wild Creations did not come easily, and indeed he went through many phases of regret and doubt initially. In the end, however, he emerged a "changed" man, arguably "calloused," much like one emerges after having his/her heart broken a few times, with much more fortitude and resolve to face the challenges again and with much more confidence.

Whether you believe you can learn to be an entrepreneur or are born with the necessarily "gene," the first question that needs to be considered is this: Do you even want to be one?

Interestingly, a 2011 survey conducted by the insurance company, AFLAC, found that seventy-five percent of Americans would prefer self-employment to working for someone else. Some may find this number low; others may find it high. Regardless, more interesting is the fact that, even with three quarters of Americans preferring self-employment, only six percent of Americans are actually engaged in entrepreneurship, according to recent data from the Bureau of Labor statistics.

Why the disparity between the number of people who want to be entrepreneurs and the number of people actually pursuing it?

There are many factors the explain the difference: lack of startup capital, inexperience, no support from family to make it happen. Some are stuck in "job lock," or the idea that having benefits at their current job, such as health insurance or a long-term vested pension plan, are holding them back from leaving. Still others fear failure, sacrificing their credit score, or ultimately filing bankruptcy. While all of these are valid reasons worthy of consideration, they are excuses rooted in a single and incredibly crucial personal trait.

Confidence.

Confidence, however, is a tricky and manipulative beast. The societal paradigm is to believe that in order to be an entrepreneur, one needs to have the confidence and unfaltering fortitude of a stonewall, requiring complete and unwavering faith in yourself and your abilities. This is a lot to swallow in one spoonful, and it is enough to keep many borderline risk-takers from trying.

Confidence is not actually this complicated. The profound truth is that the ultimate test of your entrepreneurial ability is this: do you simply have the confidence to *try*? We believe if you can muster enough courage to set out on that ambition, finding the wherewithal to endure the pressure, risk, and eventual failures can be learned and refined through the proper support and knowledge you gain once you start.

How that confidence initially manifests, whether innately or through learned experience, is what we disagree on. But we both agree that once you start, everyone has the ability to succeed.

This is what we intend to prove through this book, through our unlikely backgrounds and even more unlikely entrepreneurial success and experience. We did not start Wild Creations with the confidence and fortitude of an Elon Musk or Sir Richard Branson. We simply had the confidence to try.

We were, in fact, just like most of you.

For the half of you who fall into the category of individuals who do not prefer self-employment, who enjoy the comfort and security of a steady paycheck, benefits and other perks, we are by no means saying that you lack confidence. On the contrary, your confidence to finish school or pursue a trade or succeed within a company is admirable.

Seriously, rock on.

During our most stressful early days with Wild Creations, when we were pouring ourselves physically, mentally, and emotionally into our business each and every day, we would often reminisce and long for the days of regular paychecks, turning off work at the end of the day and having weekends off.

Heck, we would even conjecture that prison, with its regular meals, full gym, library, and occasional movie night might be nice alternative to the hell we were enduring. Seriously, compared to some of the early interactions we had, dealing with a convicted murderer as a bunkmate seemed like child's play.

Of course, we jest.

For the other half of you who have dreams of entrepreneurship -- and reading this book is the first clue that you do -- then we believe you have what it takes to get started. If you have not already packed a *Bankers Box* with your *Swingline* stapler, unused *Post It* notes and cheesy three year old vacation photos and walked into your supervisor's office, resignation in hand, then read on and we will demonstrate why you should.

HOW WE STARTED

We met in 2004 while working as business and economic development consultants on a United States Aid for International Development (USAID) program. The project was based in Central Asia and focused on providing business consulting and training to the numerous small and medium-sized businesses that were only ten years removed from the fall of the Soviet Union. The project, aptly named the Enterprise Development Project (EDP), had offices in all five countries: Kazakhstan, Uzbekistan, Kyrgyzstan, Tajikistan, and Turkmenistan (cumulatively "the Stans").

Interestingly -- and ironically -- when they first met, it was not under the most amenable circumstances.

Rhett originally landed in the Central Asia as a Peace Corps Volunteer in 2000. Prior to this, he was a blossoming executive in radio management. When he met and married his wife (not simultaneously), they decided to uproot, sell everything, and have an adventure. While most people would not consider the Peace Corps a great honeymoon choice, it was exactly the type of adventure they loved and needed.

Their Peace Corps assignment landed them in the gorgeous and historic city of Bukhara, Uzbekistan, where he taught business at the local university and consulted several small tourism companies. Their stay was cut short just thirteen months later when all U.S. personnel were evacuated following the terrorist events of September 11, 2001. Rhett returned to Central Asia in October of that year to manage a USAID business development program in Tajikistan, which was just coming out of a long civil war.

Pete found his way to Central Asia as a volunteer for the MBA Enterprise Corps (now Pyxera Global), an organization similar to the Peace Corps, that placed graduate MBA students in development projects to work with other small and medium-sized businesses. Having just graduated from Georgetown University with his MBA in 2003, he accepted a unique offer from the MBA

Enterprise Corps to move to Central Asia for one year and work as a volunteer for USAID's EDP. Seeking an adventure himself, he packed a bag (which was really all he had) and landed in Almaty, Kazakhstan.

Pete fell in love with the work, the people, the culture, and the lifestyle, and when his year was up, he lobbied for a full-time position to stay. At that time, the current Kazakhstan Country Director (the individual responsible for all project operations in country) had announced he was departing. Having been based in Almaty, Kazakhstan, during his assignment, and given the fact that the departing Kazakhstan Country Director was a former MBA Enterprise Corps volunteer (as was the Kazakhstan Country Director befor him), Pete seemed an obvious (at least in his mind) choice to fill the vacant position. If nothing else, the job should be his by virtue of legacy.

Enter Rhett.

Unbeknown to Pete, the EDP had hired Rhett to replace the outgoing Kazakhstan Country Director. When the news was shared in the Almaty office that summer of 2004, the introduction was made as, "Hey everyone, this is Rhett, the new Kazakhstan Country Director."

What Pete heard was, "This is the asshole who just took your job."

To add insult to Pete's injured pride, they both shared the same small office, with five others, and had desks just a few feet away. For a short time, while finishing up his volunteer assignment, Rhett was Pete's boss.

It all turned out fine, and Pete ended up with a position as the Finance Consulting Director, which not only provided him the freedom and opportunity to travel to all of the project offices throughout the region, but also offered the opportunity to create, implement and manage a consulting practice from scratch, an experience and challenge he thrived on. Pete later moved to Turkmenistan where he assumed the Country Director role for the project.

We eventually became good friends and would frequent bars and restaurants, drink beer, eat pizza, and talk. To the best of our recollection, it was over this pizza and beer, in a dimly lit Georgian restaurant high in the Tian Shan Mountains of Kazakhstan, that the idea of starting a business was seeded.

"Hey man, I got it! Let's sell frogs!"

"Duuuude! You are a GENIUS! Gimme another beer."

Okay, not exactly. Our ambitions were not rooted in the idea of starting a frog company. In fact, it did not happen with one particular idea or in one given moment but instead over a period of many visits (and many pizzas and many beers).

Our overseas work had brought us together, but our entrepreneurial ambitions fueled the connection and the conversation. We would often lament about the trivial politics of our jobs and how to solve the world's problems, but the conversation always gravitated to starting and running a business. We started to realize that we were both passionate about building something, and we were infatuated with the "image" of being entrepreneurs -- freedom, wealth, and influence. We were smart, we were connected, and we were wildly ambitious.

We were also overly confident and naive.

We continued to talk about starting a business but continued to pour ourselves into our consulting jobs. We would then complain that we were pouring ourselves into our jobs and not starting a business. This went on for months.

Eat. Drink. Complain. Repeat.

The catalyst came in 2005, shortly after Pete had accepted a position as the Turkmenistan Country Director and moved to Ashgabat, Turkmenistan. We continued to talk by phone and, when Country Directors met during monthly retreats, would spend evenings carrying on the conversation.

Later that year, Rhett had made his second trip to Afghanistan as part of a management group of consultants who were to consult USAID in country. A few days after arriving in Kabul, Rhett called Pete.

> **Pete:** I remember that phone call. It was a Saturday morning, and Rhett called at some ungodly early time -- 11AM, I think -- and started the conversation by saying, "I got bombed last night." In my sleepiness, I remember spending the first few minutes asking him about where he went and how much he had to drink. You know -- how did you get *bombed* (drunk)? I couldn't stop laughing at him.
>
> As the fogginess cleared, Rhett finally stressed to me that he had actually been bombed, as in mortar shells exploding all around him. His complex in Afghanistan had been attacked with mortars. That was an eye-opener for me. And I know it was for Rhett, as well, given he and his wife were expecting their second kid. It's easy to see this was the point where the two of us decided it was time to act, once and for all, to start a business. Stop talking about it and just do it -- before one of us gets killed.
>
> **Rhett:** I remember that call as well. We were having this in-depth, gut-check conversation. It wasn't so much about settling down. It was more or less about wanting. I had options for my future. I could have quit and taken a job with a desk, have a good salary, and have a good life. That would have been easy.
>
> The thing was, I had been there, done that. I wanted something more. It was about never wanting to be on my death bed saying, "I didn't do stuff. I didn't try things. I didn't experience

> life." I wasn't going to be one of those people -- I know a lot of them -- who sit at a job for thirty years and then retire. For me, it was time to live, make a go of it, and go forward, believing in myself that I could accomplish anything. Pete believed in that, too. We knew going into business was the right thing to do and it was the right time.

Our ambitions were always clear, but it took the Afghan War to push us to act. So what will be your motivation?

ARE YOU AN ENTREPRENEUR?

Make no mistake about it, entrepreneurship involves risk -- financial, emotional, and even physical. There is intense stress and anxiety involved and, to a lesser extent, actual physical threats (ex-employees, boyfriends of ex-employees, customers -- it happens).

Entrepreneurship weighs heavily on personal relationships as well, particularly family and friends, and when you start factoring opportunity cost into the equation, especially if you are comfortably in a career and well-paying job with benefits, it's all enough to give anyone indigestion.

Natural born entrepreneurs have an innate ability to mitigate fear and doubt when engaging in risk taking. They don't eliminate it altogether by any means, but instead have the ability to minimize it and focus on the bigger picture. More important, this ability is developed over time and with experience, as is any skill that requires practice.

Even if you don't believe you have that innate ability to minimize the fear and doubt with excessive risk, we believe you can develop that skill through learned experience -- as long as you are willing to try.

With that said, it is important to fully understand what we believe are the necessary characteristics of successful entrepreneurs before you even set out. Consider the following thought exercises, which are meant to provide a few elementary scenarios, especially early on. Like a self-defense class, if you continue to practice and visualize these situations, before they happen, you will be better prepared to react properly when they do.

Thought Exercise 1

Imagine you are steering a massive ship down a narrow river, with extremely valuable cargo aboard, and you come to an unplanned fork in the river. You don't know what lies ahead in any direction, and you understand that once committed, you cannot turn back. Can you handle that kind of decision making, or do you opt to ask another individual to decide, maybe one who you can later blame if it is the wrong decision?

Now imagine that the fork has 5 different directions. Now imagine it has 50.

If you believe you can handle situations that call for incredibly difficult decision-making with completely unknown outcomes, and if you believe you are willing to accept complete responsibility for the potential failures of those decisions, this is a significant leadership trait needed to be an entrepreneur. Maybe you believe you can handle the decision making, but you hate the stress associated with that kind of responsibility? As we've stated, the ability to mitigate the fear and stress comes with time. The fact that you have the fortitude to take chances and accept responsibility is just the start.

Thought Exercise 2

Imagine you receive a job offer from the company with which you have always wanted to work, but the salary is much lower than what you expected. They tell you that nobody is hired with a higher salary than people who have worked there for many years, but the opportunity for growth and success is limited only by your willingness to work hard. Now, imagine you receive another job offer that will pay twice as much, but it is from a company not nearly as desirable. Which do you choose?

Are you the type of person who prioritizes opportunity, often at the expense of wealth, because you understand you are in charge of your own success, and opportunity is all you need to reach that potential? Entrepreneurs do not necessarily endeavor into business to get rich. In fact, a majority of the entrepreneurs you will meet start and run businesses in order to build something they can call their own. Something they can stick a flag in. A legacy.

Most entrepreneurs are not content with living vicariously through the rich idiots on television reality shows. Their dreams are not delusions of grandeur seeded in an occasional lottery ticket or a perfect March Madness bracket. They don't wait for someone to come up and hand them their opportunities, their fortunes, their lives. They understand that wealth and happiness come through self-fulfillment, which can only be achieved through their efforts.

Thought Exercise 3

Imagine you are asked to skip a paycheck to float a company while you wait for a big contract to be concluded. Is your first thought about missing your rent/mortgage payment or 401(k) contribution? Or do you instantly think of ways you can navigate around the upcoming bills in order to buy yourself a little time?

Now, imagine being asked to move out of your apartment, take a second mortgage, or cash in that 401(k) in order to keep the company afloat until the contract is signed.

If your goals in life go beyond a hefty balance in the bank, a mansion with more rooms than you can count, or a perfect credit score, and if you understand that fulfillment in life goes beyond material wealth, then it will be much easier for your to operated under the conditions of running your own business.

The third consideration is really important. We are by no means saying that wealth should not be your motivation for being an entrepreneur. Absolutely, wealth is and should be a goal and motivator -- but not by itself. Balancing the desire for wealth with risk tolerance and acceptance of your own fate is what weaves the fabric of entrepreneurship. Entrepreneurs are rarely successful once. They succeed -- then they fail -- then they succeed again -- then they fail catastrophically -- then they dig their way back to even -- fail -- succeed -- and so on. All along they way, they become better at assessing risk and managing stress and, hence, become better decision makers and better dealing with the stress.

That experience is what leads to wealth.

ENTREPRENEURIAL MOTIVATIONS

Many people talk about the freedoms that come with being one's own boss, which is a type of wealth for some people. Of course, if your idea of freedom is *free time* for vacation and travel, you may be grossly overestimating what freedom means in terms of entrepreneurship.

Entrepreneurial freedom means being free from the burden of blaming others for your failures. It means being free from depending on someone or something else for your own happiness. It means being completely liberated from the societal measures of wealth and success.

It is a freedom that says, "If I get out of bed today and bust my ass, I'm going to be happy."

More important than wealth and time, your motivation should come from something deep down inside you. It is a motivation rooted in self-drive.

"I can be more than I am."

"I haven't reached my true potential."

"I want to accomplish something."

"I want to be remembered for something significant."

"I am tired of simply making a living. I want to feel alive."

If thoughts like these permeate your thoughts and actions every day, you are an entrepreneur. Period.

More than likely, however, your drive is in constant conflict with inner reservations that hold you back.

"I could fail and go bankrupt. It would ruin my credit."

"I haven't saved enough in my 401(k) to retire yet."

"I need medical insurance."

"I could work myself into an early grave."

"I'd never see my spouse or kids."

"I can't afford it."

We are absolutely certain you have had one or more or all of these thoughts at some point in your career. We hear these and a number of other "excuses" time and time again. While these concerns are certainly valid to you, we are here to tell you that they are rooted in and perpetuated by societal paradigms that exist in a false reality, which we will explain later.

It is probably worthy to note if you choose to venture out and start a business because you hate your job or your boss, or because you find yourself in the unfortunate circumstance of being unemployed or underemployed, proceed with caution. This motivation alone is not enough to start. This is particularly true if you have a marketable skill or expertise and might be prone to take on the next stable employment opportunity.

Let's be honest. Because starting a business is tough, relentlessly tiresome, and stressful, it will be extremely tempting to stop (or as most say, "postpone") your business ambitions as soon as a lucrative and stable job offer presents itself.

Imagine you are struggling to get your business started. You're working 15 hours a day and eating Ramen noodles at every meal. One day, a recruiter phones and offers you an opportunity to interview for a high-paying job with benefits. What are you going to do?

In the end, even after running numbers and considering the numerous variables and opportunity costs associated, a truly driven entrepreneur will not delay their self-employment ambitions, but someone who started with the wrong motivations most likely will.

If you are uncertain how you would react in this situation, don't fret. It's a completely natural doubt to have. When we started, we were "lucky" enough to be starting a business during one of the worst economic recessions of a generation; there weren't any jobs available for a couple of middle-aged business consultants -- or any jobs in general -- so we were never tempted with stability as an alternative.

What we can tell you now with great certainty is, knowing what we now know, starting and running a business was one of the most fulfilling and rewarding experiences of our professional careers -- and our lives. As we have and continue to endeavor to start new businesses, we understand that even a dream job with a dream company and a dream salary can never compare to the rewards of running your own business.

Entrepreneurship is that dream job.

Of course, without that experience under your belt, we completely understand that doubt will still linger, and how you react to the temptation of stability is still unknown. One thing you can do to help you stay on course, however, is to fully understand, and write down, your expectations.

SETTING EXPECTATIONS

We have discussed that the "secret" to succeeding at entrepreneurship does not necessarily lie in a biological gene or magical formula of fortitude and hard work. Indeed, it lies in the simple task of just trying. Success, like dominoes, is a series of experiences that need to happen after the endeavor has started, and it is these experiences that refine your skills and ability to achieve succeed.

Additionally, your measure of success should not be simply wealth, material possessions, or more time to enjoy life, but instead the lessons and experiences garnered through the trials and tribulations, successes and failures of your entrepreneurial journey.

Before you write that letter of resignation or fill out a business loan application, here are few tips to get you started on setting the proper expectations. Start by thinking about and writing down your expectations, keeping in mind that while they should be fluid and flexible, your goal of entrepreneurial independence should not.

1. **List your professional and personal interests.** This will help you focus and find a business that will provide the greatest happiness and hence the greatest chance for overcoming challenges and enduring failures. Be honest and list everything you enjoy. This is the time to set a high bar with interests about which you are passionate, because passion and perseverance are directly related. What you do not want to list are careers or industries that are "safe." If you love accounting, then starting and

running an accounting firm is probably a passion. If you think accounting is a safe industry with strong demand, then get a job as an accountant. You don't want to put your time and energy into a business that does not interest you and make you happy, no matter how stable and lucrative it might be.

2. **List your skills, strengths and weaknesses.** Whether you have a specific skill or are a "jack of all trades, master of none," it is important to understand your strengths and weaknesses. This is not the time for prideful naivete ("I suck at nothing"). Instead, be humble and painfully honest with yourself. Not only will an understanding of your strengths and weaknesses be of great value when looking for business opportunities, it will allow you to identify the partners you need to make your company successful.

3. **List your personality traits.** It is easy to lump personality traits into skill strengths and weaknesses, but they should not be. They are the framework for all of the other considerations you make. Do you thrive while working in teams or on your own? Are you introverted or extroverted? Do you get along with one type of personality more than others? Understanding the type of person you are and, hence, the type of entrepreneur you will be is important for understanding the business, industry and teams with which you will work. Identifying your personal traits can be challenging for some people, but this should not be a time for prideful ignorance. Miscalculations in this regard can derail your efforts quickly. For instance, if you believe you are a great and inspirational leader of teams, but in reality you are difficult to work with, then you might realize, much too late, that you are in the wrong business. You might also consider asking your family, friends and colleagues for honest feedback.

4. **List what you are and are not willing to risk.** This is not as obvious as it may sound. Unless you ask yourself, honestly, what you are willing to lose, you might not understand what is truly at risk. For instance, it is easy to say that you are not willing to risk the IRA or 401(k) you have spent the better part of your career building. However, when you consider that your business is your retirement opportunity, and that your money sitting in retirement accounts, earning five percent annually, could be much, much better managed if invested in your business, then cashing out that 401(k) will seem like a logical idea. As you start your business, banks and investment partners will want to know you are risking as much as them, so being prepared mentally for that sacrifice makes it much easier to continue in the process when those hurdles are reached.

5. **List the time you are willing to commit.** Think long and hard about this. Whatever you estimate may be -- number of hours per day, per week or per month -- multiply that estimate by ten. Then, add one full day. Starting a business requires an incredible amount of time, and if you have certain obligations that are absolute, you need to prepare for them. For example, you may determine that due to religious reasons you cannot work during the certain holidays. You should not, therefore, pursue a business that operates during peak holiday seasons, such as a retail store or service, because with complete and absolute certainty, you will work during the holidays. Another very important consideration is family. How much time you are able to spend on the business will be greatly influenced by the support you receive from your family. Be sure to have this conversation with all family stakeholders.

6. **List the amount of income you need to make.** Actually, what you are considering is how much money you need to survive. When you make a financial budget, it is important

to understand that, unless the expense is crucial for your physical survival, you should not consider it as a priority in your business. For instance, budgeting for dining out, magazine subscriptions, bi-weekly haircuts, etc may seem like something that you need to include, but when push comes to shove, you have two primary needs: shelter and food. Growing your business with as little debt and dependence as necessary requires a good deal of re-investment in your business. At some point in the business, when all cylinders are firing, it will be much more feasible to include a gym membership or flying lessons into your budget. From the onset, however, be prepared to dedicate every dollar and ounce of energy to the business.

In the end, writing things out is more about having a brutally honest and, to a certain extent, philosophical conversation with yourself about your expectations. We will emphasize again and again that endeavoring to be an entrepreneur requires time, energy and resources, and much more than is typically expected. If you have the wrong expectations, when challenges arise, you will be less prepared to make the difficult decisions.

Rhett: Pete and I believed from the very beginning that we wanted to build and grow a successful company and be international. From our early days in Central Asia, we dreamed and thought big. There's nothing wrong with being a small business in a small town, but we wanted to be something else. You can accomplish whatever you want to if you dream and think big enough, but you will never get there if you don't understand the sacrifices required.

With the nature of our partnership and who we are, we did not want to be confined to anything. We understood that you can't grow a business without taking risks, but we also understood that we wouldn't take risks unless we had a clear expectation of what we could lose.

Pete: Not all entrepreneurs want to be a large, multinational business. Some just want to run a successful local printing franchise or family ice cream restaurant. They want to keep it simple so they can spend time coaching their kid's baseball or soccer team. Not only is that okay -- that's outstanding. It's all about expectations.

For us, we never wanted to start a business simply to make a living. We wanted to start and grow something of significance. We may not have known how we were going to do it at first, but we knew the scale of what we wanted to achieve. Because that was our expectation, and because we understood what was at risk, difficult and emotional decisions were a little easier to swallow when they came up. For instance, when the financial crisis hit us and we needed cash, we never questioned the decision to cash out our 401(k) accounts to keep us going. Finding success starts with setting expectations.

CHAPTER TWO

If you're not a risk taker,
you should get the hell out of business.

-- Ray Kroc, Founder, McDonald's

WE GET STARTED

With our expectations set and the decision to get started behind us -- or more aptly, after we concluded that starting a business was a safer option than getting shot in Afghanistan -- the next logical step was to determine what we wanted to do. It was early 2006, and Rhett had returned to his home in Columbia, South Carolina, for the birth of his second son. Pete was finishing up the USAID project and transitioning the EDP office in Turkmenistan to local managers.

Our original vision, which we had started developing prior to departing Central Asia, was to create a holdings company, originally called Nomad Partners -- yes, aptly named from our time in Central Asia -- that would build and manage a portfolio of companies that were undervalued or underperforming. We would seek companies through bankruptcy attorneys, accountants and banks, and our goal was to leverage our business development training and our extensive network of business professionals and apply them to these companies. The strategy was simple: identify opportunity, buy the company, reorganize the business, bring in new staff, exit wealthier than we were when we started.

We were going to start the next Berkshire Hathaway.

Of course, we needed money to pull this off, but this is where we believed we had a unique opportunity. We knew from our experience with USAID that most expats were paid well and had limited expenses, and therefore typically had hefty savings. We were going to leverage our contacts to create an investment fund that would help us buy or invest in the companies we identified for the portfolio.

We had the experience. We had the professional network. We had a rich and untapped money source. What could go wrong?

The next step was to engage in an aggressive fundraising campaign to raise capital for Nomad Partners. Pete created an extensive business and operating plan, and we had (or thought we had) covered the complex legalities associated with collecting and managing an investment fund with our own Internet research and self-generated legal documents.

We even had a cool logo.

Go figure, nobody wanted to dish over cash to a couple of guys who were starting -- but had zero experience running -- a complex investment fund. It quickly became apparent that before we could fundraise effectively, we needed to prove our business model with one or two businesses of our own.

We needed street cred.

BODIES, BUGS, AND EBENEZER SCROOGE

Pete eventually returned to the US later in 2006 and joined Rhett in Columbia, South Carolina. Originally, South Carolina was very low on the list of desirable states in which to settle and start a business. Readily available research showed that the state's neighbors -- North Carolina, Georgia, and Tennessee -- were attracting significantly more direct business investment. The difference was so vast, in fact, that Central Asia even seemed more welcoming to small businesses.

After a good amount of consideration, we ultimately found Columbia to be a great place to start, because 1) Rhett had a solid network in South Carolina, 2) the cost of living was very affordable, and 3) we saw a great opportunity to be the proverbial big fish in this small pond.

Between the two of us, we had saved enough money to make a go at is, so we secured office space in West Columbia and called it our headquarters. The space was, to say the least, in a bad part of town. It was comfortable, remarkably cheap, and as long as we left before dark, it was safe. But to give you an idea of how bad it was, consider that we were able to secure almost all of our office furniture from other offices in the building -- because all of the offices had been vacated quickly leaving behind desks, chairs and tables, as if a sudden zombie apocalypse had befallen the city.

These are the sacrifices you make when starting up, or so we told ourselves.

While we could have started our own company from scratch, we decided to pursue the acquisition of an existing company, and did so for a few reasons:

1. We wanted to focus our limited capital on purchasing an existing company that had an established client base and immediate cash flow from which we could draw and reinvest into other businesses.

2. We wanted an existing business to serve as our "flagship" company, serving our larger goal of creating a portfolio of value-oriented companies.

3. We could not decide on what we wanted to do.

We started our business search with business brokerages. In general, this is not the best place to start, because business brokers are essentially car salesmen, and the businesses they represent are more often lemons than gems. They work on commission, so they are highly incentivized to get the highest price for the business. This does not bode well for buyers.

With that said, we approached these relationships cautiously.

To our surprise, one of the first and most promising companies we were introduced to was through a business broker. The business had a long and stable history, with essentially a monopoly for its service in the Carolinas. It was generating significant cash flow with growing revenues, and because the owner had been running the business for years and wanted to retire, his price was very reasonable. Criteria-wise, it was the perfect company.

The company: a dead body removal service.

It turns out that South Carolina is highly regulated when it comes to dead body removal (as most states are). This particular company had contracts with all of the hospitals and morgues in South Carolina and North Carolina, so whether the corpse was being transported from one location to another, being peeled from the pavement after a drunk driving accident, or removed from a bathtub after dying of natural causes two weeks prior, this dead body removal service was the company you called.

From a business standpoint, if you were dead somewhere in the Carolinas, these folks got the call. It was a nice business model.

This also got us thinking. Baby-boomers were reaching retirement age, in very large numbers, and a great deal of them were retiring in warmth and sun of South Carolina. You can see where this logic goes. It may sound cold and calculating, considering we are talking about someone's grand pappy or nana, but we ran the numbers. The company was already a steal for the cash flow it was generating, but when we considered the potential growth of future cash flows (that MBA paid off), this was a no-brainer.

Pete: When we first met this guy, at our broker's office, he was very excited to see two, young and ambitious guys interested in taking over his business. I was busy plugging away at numbers and envisioning myself as the dispatcher back in the office, taking phone calls, managing the place, and cashing the checks. He continued to tell us about the company and how it worked, and then he told us how excited he was to take us out on our "first call". When I heard this, it dawned on me that, yeah, from time to time, when someone calls in sick or doesn't show up for work, I'd be the guy who would have to fill in. I'd be the guy who had to remove -- and clean -- the corpse.

After that lovely thought set in, I started to review his inventory list, which consisted of stainless steel carts, numerous body bags, an unmarked white van with dark tinted windows, and two "scrapers". At first, I couldn't figure out what "scrapers" meant, but then it dawned on me -- "body scrapers." You had to have someway to get the dead body up off of the pavement, I supposed. I zoned out of the rest of that meeting.

Rhett: The one thing we hadn't considered about the body retrieval company, other than the total gross-out factor, was this guy ran it as a home business, and we'd have to as well. There was no official office location. There were going to be periods of time -- on the weekends, for example, when the morgues were closed -- that we would have to store the bodies. They had to go somewhere. After all, it's the south, and it's warm, and -- well, use your imagination.

My wife and I had just bought a house and moved in with our kids. There was no way I could see myself saying to her, "Oh, honey, by the way, instead of a Jacuzzi or pool or tricked-out swing set in the backyard, we have to build a cold-storage morgue." Yeah, that wasn't going to happen. But man, the business had cash flow.

Needless to say, we didn't buy a dead body removal company. We did, however, have a new and critical criterion for other businesses that we would consider.

Over the next few months, we continued to interview business owners and assess businesses for sale.

Roofing Company: A roofing company with growing revenues and, with the housing market booming, a growing client base. More important, it had been 20 years since Hurricane Hugo crushed the Carolina coast, leaving tens of thousands of homes in need of repair. Those repairs were now 20 years old and ready to be replaced. Timing and potential was great -- but we weren't roofers, so when needed, neither of could get on a roof and lay shingles.

Rain Gutter Company: A strong company with a large client base, but the owner was not willing to part with the intellectual property -- a patented gutter system -- which was the most appealing part of the deal. Additionally, we just could not get passionate about rain gutters.

Pet Store: A small pet store that was having significant financial problems. Our market research revealed very limited competition in the area, but the market was large and growing, so it seemed a great candidate for our turn-around expertise. Ultimately, we concluded it would take much more working capital to get started than we had. Also, Pete is allergic to cats.

Pest Control Company: A solid company with a repeating and growing client base and overly-excited owner. The housing market, at this time, was exploding, and with a previous career as a Purchasing Director for a large home builder, Pete thought he might be able to work a few channels and secure contracts with a new home builders in the area.

Many of the opportunities we looked at were housing based, but in the end, we looked real long and hard at the housing market and decided that something was amiss. If the housing market crashed, and we felt strongly it could, we would not be able to work on the grand vision of Nomad Partners and would instead be relegated to driving white trucks with gutters or giant plastic termites on top or doing roofing calls every weekend. Again, this was not something we could get excited about.

There were other companies, several in fact, but none we felt passionate about. We were running out of options -- and money.

Later that year, in the fall of 2006, we decided to meet a new business broker in Columbia. To say the meeting did not go as expected is an understatement of epic proportion. The broker was perhaps 60 years old, but because of his demeanor and years of self-inflicted physical neglect, he looked more like a weathered 90 year old. He was crotchety, obnoxious, and loud: a living cliché of a native New York curmudgeon. He scowled when he talked, chewed what appeared to be a cud, and reminded us on more than one occasion that he proudly survived "twunny-seven hahhht attacks." What he lacked in personality and customer service, he made up for in scornful insults.

He was the living embodiment of Ebenezer Scrooge.

Upon our first meeting, we described to him our grand vision for Nomad Partners, and our immediate goal of finding a good company with which we could instill our business development background. It did not matter which industry or type of business, as long as it met our criteria.

We explained that we were most interested in a business with potential.

Well, that is to say we attempted to explain all of this, as it was difficult to do with his insistent interrupting. Throughout it all, he berated us and spewed vile insults, eventually cutting us off completely and insisting we return only when we had decided on a specific type of company. As he ushered us out of his untidy and damp office, cursing and spewing chalky spit as we left.

It was actually very, very comical. So much so that we decided to return a couple of weeks later for a follow up meeting to see if he could berate us more. In reality, we just wanted to "poke the dragon" more and see if he might have another heart attack.

After pleasantries -- or as pleasant as conversation could be -- he flipped positions completely and, in a slightly more supportive and parental tone, started preaching that we were "too focused on one industry", going on to emphasize that we needed to be flexible in our goals. In true used-car salesman manner, he continued to butter us up, leading to what was clearly going to be a sales pitch.

And, almost certainly, a "lemon" company.

As we started to leave, he stopped us and pulled a single file out from underneath his old and faded wooden desk. He leaned forward, darted his eyes around the room as if there might be another person eavesdropping, lowered his voice and said, "I've got this aquarium company in Myrtle Beach. Good cash flow. They're desperate to get rid of it. You can get it for a really good price." He then handed the folder over like it was full of top-secret government documents.

Our immediate reaction was to laugh. After being berated and cursed for our inexplicable lack of focus, showing us a random aquarium business in a city that was three hours away was beyond demeaning. We took the file and, without giving it a second thought, tossed it in with our other documents.

After the meeting, Pete decided to use this aquarium company as an excuse (and business write off) to visit the beach for the weekend and "research" the company. He phoned and made an appointment with the owners of the business, then drove out on a Friday afternoon ready for a weekend of rest.

Pete: I drove from Columbia to Myrtle Beach on a Friday morning. It was cloudy, overcast, and chilly. Although it was late fall, it was not the weather I was hoping to find for a weekend at the beach.

I met the owners at the company warehouse after lunch. It was a typical family business -- mom kept the books, dad did deliveries, and the son did the marketing and general management. They had a quaint 2,500 square foot space with two employees.

To my surprise, it wasn't an aquarium business, or at least the aquarium business I expected. The son gave me a tour and showed me the product, which he described as a desktop ecosystem. He walked me through how they made it and how it worked. In this facility, they would create "living gravel" by taking ordinary aquarium gravel and inoculating it with -- well, that's a trade secret. Suffice it to say that the gravel would essentially create a biological filter for the water, and together with the live Chinese lucky bamboo and two aquatic African dwarf frogs created a self-cleaning and self-filtering aquarium. The more he talked, the more amazing the product sounded.

An aquarium you don't have to clean? Incredible.

There were no other products like it on the market. None. For the previous four years, they worked four months over the summer, then closed and returned to Canada for the remainder of the year. This meant the sales numbers we were provided were for a third of the year. Incredible.

He went on to explain the biggest challenge for them, and the reason why he was selling the business, was distribution. They had been driving and hand-delivering each aquarium to beachwear and gift shops in beach cities from Maryland to Florida, but because he and his wife were having children, he couldn't keep up with the schedule.

As I left, he closed by saying what this business needed was a couple of young, ambitious and business-inclined guys to take it to the next level. Clearly, we were those guys.

It was the atypical business school case study: great product, huge untapped potential market, significant barriers to entry, but with one HUGE challenge: distribution. If we could figure out how to scale and distribute, we could make this company big.

Symbolically, when I walked out of the office, I looked up at the sky and noticed the clouds had cleared, the sun was shining, and it was a gorgeous and warm day. As someone who doesn't believe in luck or fate, it was difficult to overlook the "sign."

I called Rhett and said, "I think this it! Wild Creations is our business."

WHERE DO WE GO FROM HERE

After the visit, and after a great deal of research and discussion, we decided to acquire the product and existing assets. Our excitement of finally finding a worthy business target and our general naiveté prompted us to make a full price offer, conditional only on the satisfactory completion of our due diligence. In hindsight, letting our impatience influence our buying decision was a mistake, as we should and could have certainly negotiated a better price and better terms.

Another factor that helped solidify our decision was when we attended a trade show with owner's father to see firsthand how consumers reacted to the product. He was an immigrant from Israel and had a thick accent. He loved to talk and was very excited to attend the show with us. I suspected, however, that he was more excited to have helping hands that were willing to work for free.

We attended a pet trade show, the kind you typically find in convention centers. There were easily two hundred vendors peddling everything from organic canine snacks to carpeted rabbit habitats. With so many vendors and such a variety of product offerings, we thought it was hardly a place where we would get much attention.

> **Pete**: I ran through my sales pitch with the dad, which was about a minute long. He cut me off and insisted I get it down to a few seconds. I thought he was nuts. Then, I watched as he began taping and preparing customer boxes and stacking them in the back of the booth. The boxes were for people to take away purchases. I thought it looked cluttery and wanted to have a better presentation. He kept saying, over and over, "Trust me, Peter. Trust me, Peter." It was his show, so I did what he said.
>
> When the event opened, there were people crawling over each other and crying out for our aquariums. They were literally throwing money at us. I couldn't take it from them fast enough. Most people didn't want, or need, my sales pitch. It was madness.
>
> **Rhett:** We seriously didn't have time to eat lunch. There were no breaks, not even to go to the bathroom. Customers were lined up six deep to get these aquariums. You couldn't have had a better sales pitch for the business. Seeing the way people were reacting in such a visceral way, we knew it didn't matter at all what the details of their paperwork were. We wanted this product. We figured the company was grossly under-valued and we could take it to the next level with a few tweaks.

Again, allowing our overzealous excitement influence our judgment led to us rushing into the deal. This, and a few other factors, ultimately caused us to overpay and land fewer conditions in our favor.

LET'S MAKE A DEAL

Once we were convinced this was the company we wanted to purchase, we signed a "Letter of Understanding" with the curmudgeon broker and began our due diligence. The broker turned over a few documents, but not nearly enough to paint a clear overall picture of the business. As the information began to roll in, we began to see concerning issues. For starters, the company had not reported any income on their tax returns, although they were making "hundreds of thousands of dollars." The personal expenses paid by the company were not covering the difference, so we probed and continued to ask questions.

We requested a good deal of additional information, including financials, vendor information, and purchase receipts. This prompted phone calls, often late at night, from the curmudgeon broker, who cursed us for asking. He insisted the information we were requesting was confidential and sensitive, and went on to say that if we kept asking such ignorant questions, he would kill the deal.

Unfortunately, this was our first experience with buying a business, and specifically with dealing with a business broker. In order to save money, we did not consult or hire an advisor of our own, believing we could negotiate and navigate the process by ourselves. In hindsight, this was a huge mistake, as we allowed the curmudgeon broker to control and bully us during the process.

Eventually, we were able to get important information from the owners themselves, who clearly did not want the deal to get killed. The company operated mostly on cash, and they had been reporting less income than they actually made for years. They understood that the only way we could value the business was to be transparent with the rest of the company. We were finally able to use all of the company's purchasing receipts to reverse engineer actual financials for the business and ended up valuing it at more than our agreed upon price, given the existing market conditions, of course. The cooperation from the owners allowed us to close the deal on schedule and, for the most part, to our satisfaction.

This in spite of yet another heart attack by the broker. His twenty-eighth.

Again, looking back, we should have found a trusted advisor to assist us in this first endeavor. While we were happy with the price of the company, almost certainly we could have secured a better price and better terms had we had consultation.

A broader lesson is the understanding that leverage is on the side of confidence. Constant threats of blowing up the deal kept us in check and limited the information we requested. Because we were inexperienced with negotiating and completing due diligence, we were at the mercy of an old, angry and experienced broker who, again, was incentivized to get a high price for the business. Putting our pride aside and allowing an experienced negotiator to represent us would have leveled the playing field.

If you feel that buying an existing company is better option for you than starting one from scratch, do not fret the process too much. Of course, doing so is a long and arduous ordeal, requiring a great deal of due diligence and consideration, but before you even get intimidated by all of it, here are a few tips to get you started and help you along through the process.

FINDING A BUSINESS TO BUY

1. **Business brokers:** As we discussed, business brokers are a great place to start, but you need to approach with this resource with caution. While you may "hire" a Broker to find you a business, remember their fiduciary obligation is to the sellers, who have hired them to determine the highest value for their business and to find a willing buyer.

Like car salesmen or real estate agents, they work on commissions, typically five to ten percent, so they have every reason to find the highest price for their offering.

With that said, they also have an incentive to sell -- no sale, no commission -- so you have some leverage when negotiating. During negotiations, be sure to find a price you feel is reasonable and, more importantly, you are comfortable with. Be sure to include terms and conditions you need and understand where you can compromise. If you make an offer, the broker, who may not like the deal, still has an obligation to present the deal to the seller. Most sellers are selling for a reason, so they are more likely to react positively to an offer and be willing to negotiate than a broker would be.

2. **Browse the Web:** These days, you can find anything on the Internet. Most web searches for business-for-sale will lead you to a business broker, but once in a while, you may find an owner promoting his or her company through other sites. Much like someone who tries to sell their own house, a "For Sale By Owner" is trying to avoid the hefty commission.

   These types of deals can be dangerous. Without an experienced individual to value the business and understand the complex legalities of the necessary disclosures, you might be really buying a lemon. If you decide to go around a broker, make sure you have an attorney available to help review and facilitate documents.

3. **Business attorneys and accountants.** These people work closely with business owners and may have leads on possible acquisition targets. While it is the responsibility of the attorney or accountant to maintain client privilege and protect the privacy of its clients, it does not stop you from inquiring. Although most will shun an inquiry, some may

be aware of a client interested in selling their business or who might be in financial trouble. It does not hurt to ask.

4. **Business owners:** If you identify an appealing business, it is wise just to go straight to the business owner and inquire yourself. They owner may not be interested in selling the company, but perhaps they simply had not considered it. Inquiring may plant a seed or accelerate a planned exit or retirement. And, if the owner has no interest, they may be aware of another business in the industry that is for sale.

   This approach also requires careful consideration. Approaching and inquiring directly with a business owner could be received as an indication that his or her business is highly appealing, which may lead them to ask an unreasonable price.

5. **Trade magazines and associations:** Many business magazines have classifieds listing business and franchises for sale. Some industries and trades have publications and websites specific to their industry with their own specific classifieds. Look specifically for local business publications with company owners who seem to be nearing retirement age. Keep your eyes open and investigate each lead thoroughly.

6. **Chambers of commerce:** State, city, and local chambers of commerce are a great place to connect with business and legislative leaders, and the business community in general. Join and take an active role in your local chamber of commerce, expanding your network of business professionals. You will not only learn a great deal about the business environment and community, but also about the opportunities that exist.

7. **Franchises:** Buying into a franchise can be tricky. For the most part, you are buying an extension of another company, so you will be bound by a number of restrictions

limiting what you can do in and with the business. Growing your franchise is typically only possible through purchasing another location, and many franchisors have strict guidelines for who and where they allow new franchisees to expand. As well, most franchisors will require you to sign non-compete and confidentiality agreements, which means that if you ever decided to strike out on your own, it will be very difficult to do so in the same industry.

Make no mistake about it, franchises are a great way for an aspiring business owner to get his or her feet wet, but for the purpose of this books, we will not address them.

FORM AN ADVISORY TEAM

Another very important part of the business search is to make certain that you have the necessary advisors to help you through the process. As we learned, skimping on advisory services was a mistake. Here is a list of resources with whom you will want to consult.

1. **Attorneys**: They are expensive and always seem to talk too much, but we cannot understate the value they bring to the table. Unless you are an attorney yourself, do not try to facilitate an acquisition without one. The obvious legal steps and documentation associated with buying a business are trumped only by the unobvious legal steps and documentation. An attorney will help you make since of it all.

   We hired a business attorney when we first arrived in Columbia, but because of the cost, and our naiveté in believing we could figure things out on our own, we did not depend on his services much during the acquisition of Wild Creations. His expertise would have been extremely helpful (and was missed) when we closed.

2. **Accountants**: Accountants are also pricy, but because the U.S. tax code is more complicated than quantum mechanics and String Theory, you will need one. Additionally, accountants can review financial statements, help you value your acquisition target, and more importantly, find inconsistencies and concerns. They will also help you with the initial setup of your company books, figuring in the valuation of your business. All of this, like an attorney, will benefit you greatly later.

   We found an accountant in Columbia who was just starting to grow his business, so he was excited at the prospect of being part of Wild Creations and eventually Nomad Partners. He was extremely helpful, often consulting us pro bono. In the end, we rewarded his commitment to us by hiring his firm every year to complete our business and personal taxes, even though his office was three hours away.

3. **Mentors**: If you have never negotiated the purchase of a company, finding an experienced and trustworthy mentor with this experience will benefit you greatly. In addition to helping you understand what you don't know, your mentor can validate the things you think you know.

   This was our biggest, and most painful, omission when we purchased Wild Creations. Not only was negotiating and dealing with the curmudgeon broker outright frustrating, it seemed that he was often holding back valuable information we needed for consideration. Most of the time, he would berate and curse us and threaten to kill the deal, and because we did not have an experienced individual on our side to consult, we often bowed to his pressure. With a few business acquisitions under our belt, we are certain the original negotiations for Wild Creations should have been conducted completely different.

UNDERSTANDING YOUR INDUSTRY AND COMPETITION

Experienced entrepreneurs, business coaches, and trusted mentors will all tell you to pursue what you know and love. For obvious reasons, this is great advice. To a great extent, we agree as well.

Clearly, we had no experience developing or producing ecosystem habitats, nor did we have any experience or established network in the pet or toy industries. For several years leading up to the acquisition, however, we had been working as business consultants, applying very general business practices to business of all sizes and from all industries. We were experienced with walking into a business we did not know, operating in an industry we did not know, and offering development and turnaround strategies.

We were accustomed to operating in unknown territory.

With that said, you might have a specific skill or expertise that is valuable in a variety of industries or on different scales. One of the things you need to determine prior to setting out on your entrepreneurial ambitions is what those skills are. We have said that when you list your interests and passions, think big and broad, but be realistic and make certain you have the skillset (and network and team) to lead your company to success.

In the end, we believe strongly that there are times when entering a new industry is actually beneficial, as you are not burdened with preconceived notions or biases.

We made a number of mistakes while looking for a business, both during negotiations and while conducting due diligence. Most errors were avoidable, but all were overshadowed by the immense pride we had when we signed the final deal. That same day, in fact, we drove from the closing in Columbia to the warehouse in Myrtle Beach, and with a six-pack of beer, celebrated the milestone.

As we sat in the warehouse, surrounded by boxed-up aquarium supplies, engulfed in the sounds of the large aquarium pumps, and enveloped in the pale yellow incandescent lights, we were overwhelmed with a sense of pride and accomplishment. This was our inventory. These were our aquariums. This is our business. That feeling was so profound that we both can remember where we were sitting and feeling at that very moment.

Of course, that was a fleeting moment, quickly replaced with excitement and a sense of responsibility. From that point on, we would never slow down. Our brains switched to overdrive. We had walked away from everything we had ever done in our professional lives -- politics, home building, working overseas -- and entered into a completely new realm of being. This was our baby. We were business owners. We were entrepreneurs.

We have not stopped since.

CHAPTER THREE

If you are not embarrassed by the first version of your product, you've launched too late.

-- Reid Hoffman, Venture Capitalist and Co-Founder, LinkedIn

STUFF THEY DON'T TEACH YOU IN BUSINESS SCHOOL

The whole point of business school is to groom and freshly mint talent who can run businesses and manage complex teams and systems. They provide countless tools like SWOT analysis (**S**trengths, **W**eaknesses, **O**pportunities, and **T**hreats), the 4 P's of marketing (People, Product, Packaging, Price), and the 3 C's of industry analysis (Competition, Company, Customer). More acronyms than you can find uses for.

Then, there is finance. Discounted cash flow, time value of money, managerial accounting, derivative analysis, and industry risk formulas -- enough tools and spreadsheets to make you think you were landing a rover on Mars.

When we set out on this adventure, we were pretty confident that we were ready for the challenge. We were, after all, two educated guys -- with the student loans to prove it -- who had been small business management consultants to hundreds of businesses around the world. We experience working in large and small corporations, and for non-profit and government agencies alike.

We had done our due diligence, SWOT analysis, and financial projections for our acquisition of Wild Creations, and we had integrated everything into an extensive, complex, and formulaic business plan. We were not only prepared but also fairly certain we knew exactly how our business would play out.

The day we had closed on the acquisition, we drove to the beach to visit our new business with a six pack of beer. We sat at an aging deck table in worn out plastic chairs and popped open a couple of cold frosty bottles. As we glanced around the warehouse, breathing in the damp air with pride, we clinked bottles and cheered to our new endeavor.

We were ready to roll.

FLOODS, BEER, POKER, AND BUBBA WITH A GUN

One of the doctrines taught in business school says every problem you encounter in the corporate world can be broken down, analyzed, and resolved with some four-by-four matrix. In the context of the classroom and applied to case study after case study, it works out really great.

What business school failed to provide was the four-by-four matrix and ability to break down, analyze, and resolve an issue with a scruffy business neighbor with an anger complex, whose work attire included camo pants and a hunting cap and whose office decorations included a rifle collection and hunting pictures.

Think Duck Dynasty.

The first month of the business went fairly well, although we were constantly being hit with unforeseen problems and unforeseen costs -- at least unforeseen in our complex business plan. A delivery driver running over our mailbox, a broken toilet, faulty wiring for the office, and a overly frugal landlord with his own gun collection.

As the problems and costs started to rack up, so did the stress. Nothing was going as planned. Our financial projections had not considered all of these additional costs, and we were already bootstrapped as it was. Even though we had budgeted for "contingencies," we had covered most of the expenses in a detailed budget. The pinnacle of the problems (to that point) occurred after about a month.

It is worthy to first set the scene. The primary component of Wild Creations is called living gravel (which we later trademarked as "Living Gravel" -- very original), an organic gravel that acts as a filter system for the ecosystem. It is ordinary aquarium gravel inoculated with two different strains of healthy bacteria. When we acquired Wild Creations, we inherited four very large, stainless steel aquariums that treat the gravel and housed the live aquatic frogs and, at that time, fish. In each stainless steel vessel, the gravel was kept in a bottom bin while several large, forty-gallon aquariums were positioned over it. The live frogs and fish used in the EcoAquarium stayed in these aquariums, and the entire system was on a circulating pump that ran day and night.

The challenge with these aquariums was they did not have a drainage system -- that is to say that they did not have one hooked up -- which was an oversight of the previous owner and which we neglected to correct promptly. For this reason, it was essential to make certain that any time water was added to the vessels, it was crucial to shut it off before leaving in the evening. Water left on would overflow.

You can see where this is going.

One night, we had unintentionally left the water running in one of the vessels all night. It overflowed, probably for hours, flooding the entire warehouse with several inches of standing water. Because we were in the middle of series of connected facilities, the water seeped into our next-door neighbor's office.

When we walked in the next morning, it was immediately clear that we had a flood. We quickly grabbed mops, the ShopVac and anything that soaked up water. It was slow and seemingly futile.

Almost as soon as we started, a large and imposing man stormed through the front door hollering. It was our neighbor from the adjacent warehouse, a true, gritty good-ol'-boy. His entire warehouse and office had been soaked, and his carpet and office furniture had been wrecked. He fumed, screamed, and shook his fist as we hurriedly tried to cajole him and remove the water as quickly as possible.

The primary issue -- as we discovered later -- was that our neighbor and the previous Wild Creations owner had never gotten along. They were, in fact, bitter antagonists. Unfortunately for us, our gritty neighbor had not been in his office much, so he was not aware that we had acquired the business. Our first meeting, therefore, was on these bad terms and with him demanding blood.

And of course, we did not have a contingency plan for water removal, property damage, and an irate neighbor with an anger management issue.

> **Pete:** At that point, I was already completely stressed about the business. When I went next door to see the damage, I noticed the man's impressive gun rack on the wall, surrounded by numerous hunting photos. Of all the guys we had to piss off, we had to irk the one who had a rifle collection that he clearly used liberally.
>
> After that, I quickly walked out and around to the side of the warehouse, sat down on a concrete parking bumper, and had a panic attack -- the first in my life. I thought the business was done, and we were going to have to close. We had no way to pay for the damages or the cleanup, and now we were in the crosshairs of a proud redneck.

It was a mess, but I got my wits about me and called a fire and water damage company. They came out, sucked out all the water and put huge fans inside the warehouse for drying.

Rhett: Although the guy ran an electric contracting business, he used this warehouse for a number of questionable "businesses." It had a full kitchen and a living room that doubled as a bedroom. We later found out that he would rent this space from time to time to random people for short stays. We even suspected that he used it for "working women."

Also, typically late at night, he would run a high-stakes poker game, so our parking lot would fill completely with countless 4X4 trucks with gun racks. Pete and I drove Hondas, so you could almost smell the contempt in the air on those nights. Our neighbor was just a good ole boy who didn't take kindly to anything non-U.S.A.

Pete: As the mess was being cleaned up, Rhett talked with our neighbor. As soon as Rhett mentioned he grew up in South Carolina, our neighbor toned down the rhetoric and actually warmed up to us. He even invited us to play poker. I was flattered, but broke, so I declined. Later that day, I went to the store and bought a case of Bud Light and several plug-in air fresheners and delivered the goods to his office manager. He had a poker game that night, and I explained that I hoped this would help them overlook the dampness and smell.

After that offering, we never heard from him again, even after flooding his place at least two more times.

EXPECTING THE UNEXPECTED

The run in with Bubba (the name we affectionately gave him) affirmed that we needed to expect the unexpected but also that we needed to develop the skills necessary to deal with the unexpected. The problem with most business plans like ours is that while they allow for a few contingencies, there is no way to plan for everything. Few businesses end up following their plan to the letter -- life doesn't work that way. You can have the perfect budget and the perfect strategy, be insured to the hilt, but it only takes one case of Murphy's Law, or in this case redneck rage, to throw the entire thing into a death spiral.

This is not pessimism. This is just life.

What you need to know is your resolve and ability to shift, think, and resolve unforeseen issues are far more critical than matrices, SWOT analyses, and DCFs. If you have the ability to overcome real world problems, developing a business plan becomes much less an integral part of running a business.

A REALLY BIG MURPHY

After the "Bubba Affair", the business continued to run into issue after issue. For a year, we plugged away and slowly worked at growing the business. After a few more months, we started to get a handle on the business and were getting into a groove. We had survived and kept the doors opened, and dealing with unforeseen issues became increasingly easier.

By the holiday season and well into 2008, news and concern of a softening housing market started to intensify. Many of the speculations we had about the housing market while searching for businesses were starting to permeate finance and business television shows. As the reports grew grimmer, so did the sentiments of shoppers, and nowhere was this more evident than at the small retail kiosks we were managing at the time.

In September 2008, the unthinkable happened. Lehman Brothers filed bankruptcy.

To emphasize how important an event this was, consider the fact that Lehman Brothers was a 150-year-old financial institution and the fourth-largest investment bank in the U.S. They managed over 600 billion dollars and were influential in every industry driving the economy. It was a huge deal.

When Lehman threw in the towel, everything changed.

Everyone was screwed.

> **Pete:** Wild Creations and its frog aquariums was to be one of the many companies in our holdings portfolio. Our initial strategy for Nomad Partners to continue buying undervalued companies we could improve required capital. Although our goal was to establish a reputation as business savants to be able to raise money, when Lehman Brothers collapsed, we realized quickly that, for quite a while anyway, there was not going to be any more money available to us. We were going to be a frog company, and we were going to have to rely on the frogs to survive.

We watched the whole financial debacle unfold on television. CNBC, Bloomberg TV, CNN, Fox Business News, and every pundit was reporting as if it was the end of the U.S. dollar and our economic dominance in the world.

For us, we had just bought an under-capitalized retail business and were seemingly steering it into the worst economic crisis since the Great Depression.

Talk about a depressing outlook.

To add insult, we had already maxed-out our credit, buying four new vehicles and leveraging every business and personal credit card we had. We started watching our cash flow much closer and focusing it on only those liabilities we needed to stay opened. We would pay down credit cards with just enough money to place orders with our vendors, and we would rotate those payment with each credit card as to constitute our monthly payment.

In one instance, we made a significant payment, about five thousand dollars, to a credit card in order to buy inventory. Instead of clearing the card and having the funds available to use, the credit card company lowered our limit by that exact amount. Just like that, five thousand dollars right out the window.

It was a terrible time to be an undercapitalized startup retail business.

From that point on, we were forced to make minimum payments to the cards, often late, and started doing business in cash, through overnighted checks and bank wires.

Cash was truly king.

FLYING BY THE SEAT OF YOUR PANTS

Business schools and textbooks never tell you what to do when faced with the next global economic financial crisis. When it happens, entrepreneurial survival comes down to your ability to look beyond acronyms, 4x4 matrices and spreadsheets to find the strategy, the resources, and the resilience to persevere.

> **Rhett:** It's at this point in the life of being an entrepreneur where you learn that you're not always going to pay your bills on time. You learn how to accept it. You learn how to talk about money. You recognize that you have to bite the bullet and admit what is happening in your company. You have to make those painful and embarrassing calls, but at the same time maintain a diplomatic and confident tone: "I'm sorry, I can't pay you this month. Hang in there, though, as we are working through this time with everyone, and we will get to you."
>
> You are running your company, but you have to make sure your vendors are comfortable with you, understand your challenges and what you are doing to overcome them. Keep them in the loop, and they will work with you.

Pete: In a perfect world, your customers pay you up front for your product or service, and you have Net 90 (pay within 90 days of receiving the product/service) terms with your vendors. Of course, this never works out.

As the credit markets collapsed, nobody was giving credit. Our customers and vendors were all in the same boat as us, watching the same news, feeling the same financial pressure. I would often talk quite extensively with a new client and convince them we could only ship product if payment was received up front, especially without a history of credit with us. I would then turn around with vendors and have a long, honest conversation about why I could not pay them within the terms we had. It is all about balance and communications.

PAY YOUR EMPLOYEES FIRST

There are some expenses you cannot put off. If you are late with a credit card payment, you deal with phone calls, but your business continues to run. If you are late with a payroll, you lose every employee you have.

We were very proud of the fact that during our tenure at Wild Creations, we never missed a payroll. Not one. This typically meant sacrificing our own credit and quite often not taking a paycheck ourselves. In fact, for the first two years of the business, as we were growing and dealing with the recession, we did not take a paycheck. We instead lived from personal savings and personal credit cards.

You have to put your employees at the top of the priority list, because they are making it possible for you to even have your business.

DOING WHAT YOU HAVE TO DO

The wonderful (and frustrating) thing about entrepreneurship and running your own business is that it becomes merely an extension of you, permanent and constantly in need of attention. While we believe most aspiring entrepreneurs may be aware of this, it is impossible to truly appreciate until you actually experience it.

Much like it is entirely possible to imagine what it would be like to have a third arm, but impossible to really know unless you had one.

Yes, a third arm.

Because while it might be easy to liken your business to a pet or a child, there are those who simply do not get as emotionally attached to either. But a third arm, well that is yours, it is part of you, it goes everywhere you go, and you would do everything to keep it free from harm.

This is what your business is like.

Okay, the third arm analogy is a bit creepy, but you get the point.

Doing what you need to do for the business does not come naturally. Most of the time, it requires thinking and finding solutions that you would ordinarily never consider. Downsizing and terminating people, dipping into your personal and "untouchable" savings, forgoing a paycheck and missing your rent, not paying a credit card for several months, sleeping in your office or your vehicle.

You do whatever it takes.

Remember, as an entrepreneur, *you* are your company -- 24/7. It will live or die by the decisions you make and the actions you take. You cannot dodge responsibility or avoid problems.

In the end, entrepreneurs will grasp this realization through experience. But do not allow this to intimidate you. Again, it is the terrifying and amazing reality entrepreneurs learn and come to accept.

So that the realization is more amazing than terrifying for you, just keep these tips in mind.

1. **Prioritize.** Always prioritize the things that are going to keep the doors open. This will mean sacrificing your credit, irking business partners and stakeholders, and even putting your own welfare second. Understanding the importance of prioritizing will allow you to be better prepared when tough times roll around.

2. **Always negotiate.** Remember that everything in business is negotiable. Everything. Hone your negotiating skills and be willing to use them. Negotiating is difficult for some people, but remember that the better you negotiate, the better chances you have of growing your company, and therefore the more business you have for your partners. Everybody wins.

3. **Don't avoid those harassing and uncomfortable phone calls.** Communication is key when it comes to establishing relationships with your vendors and stakeholders. You come to understand as an entrepreneur that most of your partners are just like you, so they will appreciate your honesty when it comes to your business. Whatever you do, do not over promise and under deliver, as nothing will kill your credibility faster than a check that bounces or has been "in the mail" for months.

CHAPTER FOUR

The strength of the team is each individual member.
The strength of each member is the team.

-- Phil Jackson, Legendary NBA Basketball Coach,
Chicago Bulls and Los Angeles Lakers

IT'S BETTER WITH A PARTNER

One of the most critical attributes an entrepreneur can have is strong interpersonal skills. The reason is simple: sustainable business success requires a team of employees, managers, and partners. Very few great companies are built on the strength of single entrepreneur.

Entrepreneurs therefore need to have both the talent and the charisma to convince and lead teams and stakeholders, often into wholly uncharted territory. While every successful entrepreneur has a definition or description of what this leadership skill looks like, our is quite simple:

Don't be an asshole.

Through our experiences running Wild Creations, this baseline measure has proven quite useful for measuring employees, business partners, clients, and even ourselves. We will indeed be more specific later in the chapter, but suffice it to say that if you can live up to this one criteria, you are well on your way to leading great teams and conquering small countries.

This criteria is particularly applicable when seeking out business partners. Nothing will lead your company to the brink of utter implosion faster than a terse and bitter relationship with those whom you share ownership in your business. And while it might be tempting to forego a partner altogether and seek to tackle the challenges of entrepreneurship on your own, our experience has proven that there are numerous reasons why having one or more partners is always a better alternative.

WHAT TO LOOK FOR IN A BUSINESS PARTNER

Getting started in business with a partner is tricky. In addition to finding people you trust, are financially (and mentally) stable, and have no outstanding arrest warrants -- you know, the typical criteria -- there are number of other measures you should put your potential partner up against.

Shared commitment. Entrepreneurship is not a job or a hobby; it is a commitment, one that requires passion and persistence. When the business is pitted against difficult times or significant disagreement between the partners, it is the commitment to the business that pushes the partners past the present to look to the future and dedicate the necessary time and resources to overcome any challenge. You do not want nor can you afford to have a quitter as a partner.

Shared investment. Partners need to be invested in the company, both financially and personally, and to the extent that all partners are comfortable and committed. The amount of equity assumed by every owner must be hammered out diligently before a business is even considered, as changes after the fact become very difficult and often uncomfortable to negotiate. Once the balance of fairness becomes skewed, for whatever reason, frustration and mistrust will flare and cause rifts in the partnership. Never start a business unless the details of the operations agreement, the required investment, and share of the equity are clearly spelled out.

Shared business vision. Agreement in the long-term goals of the business must be aligned between all partners. This does not necessarily imply that all partners have to agree on the specifics of products or services produced, but instead on what you all want to accomplish. Do you and your partners have a shared vision? Do you want to run a small business, which affords time to coach little league and take vacations or a diverse multinational corporation that requires extensive travel? These two ends of the spectrum have far different expectations and requirements for the business and the all partners involved. If the partners have different expectations about the time and investment required, it will cause problems.

There is no way to assess a potential partner other than with time and communication. We would not suggest posting an ad to find a business partner, but instead look into your network to find people with shared interests. Close friends and family are not always the best people with whom to partner, so look to your professional network as a great place to start looking.

You want to place particular attention on those individuals who are also interested in entrepreneurship and might even be seeking partners themselves. While it is easy to sit with a long checklist of criteria, it is nice knowing the individual you are considering is doing the same.

At the end of the day, if you find someone with the same checklist, the same expectations and the same commitments, often the other details can be worked out.

PIZZA, PEVA, AND PARTNERSHIPS

Prior to starting Wild Creations, we met while working on a USAID project in Central Asia. For three years, we became close colleagues and good friends. At the time, we did not set out to find a partner for a new business venture. We simply met after work and shared a pizza and a few peva (Russian for "beers") and talked business. For months, we yammered about how we actually enjoyed our jobs but felt unsatisfied in our careers.

As conversation topic slowly shifted to entrepreneurship, we started to realize that we had shared life goals and a similar vision about the type of company we both wanted to start. From there, the idea of partnering naturally evolved.

Before we knew it, we were talking about moving back the U.S. and getting started.

> **Rhett:** We had a shared vision for everything we wanted to accomplish, both in life and in business. We knew where we wanted to lead a company. We agreed on the big picture stuff and didn't sweat the small things. We knew we wanted to build something significant, lead teams, and ultimately build a legacy for ourselves.

> **Pete:** The idea of running a small business was never even a consideration. We knew we weren't the guys who were content playing in the minor leagues just to pay the bills. We wanted to swing hard for the fences or get cut. You can't build a legacy without growing something big, and you can't grow something big without understanding the commitment needed to do so. This was a guiding light for how we did things throughout our partnership.

BUILDING ON THE STRENGTHS OF OTHERS

The value of having partners lies in the skills and experiences each person brings to the business. One may have excellent marketing skills, while another is proficient with numbers and finances. One may be the idea generator while others are the implementers. These strengths and weaknesses cannot be assessed by sight, only through detailed conversations and setting the right expectations.

As you consider partners, be sure to discuss the goals and responsibilities of everyone involved. Each partner should have a defined role, which will be explained and detailed in the Operating Agreement (discussed later in this chapter). You all should understand, however, that while while specific responsibilities may be designated by a job description that you all have agreed to, all partners will need to contribute in other areas if and when the time calls. This is an important expectation for all to have.

Another important understanding to have is that the organization should have only one person at the top of the organization. This may be difficult for some entrepreneurs to wrap their arms around, especially when the result is allowing someone else to be the ultimate decision maker. Any partnerships, however, that tries to exist with co-presidents or co-CEOs is bound for problems. In these cases, disagreements can cause the company to come to a grinding halt as resolutions are sought.

Instead, be open and honest about each other's strengths and ambitions. Understand that all partners have authority in the organization, and large decisions affecting the organization as a whole will be made through committee. In the end, however, if consensus cannot be reached, someone has to take the leadership position and the responsibility for "pulling the trigger" and taking action.

Additionally, as the company grows and becomes more visible in your industry, having a leader at the top that is charismatic, diplomatic, and capable of communicating the vision of the company to outsiders is critical. Some entrepreneurs are simply gifted in this regard, while others prefer to take a "behind the scenes" approach to their work. Also, the company need not limit itself to one leader. As long as chemistry exists between the partners and the personality types allow it, a company can have as many public figures as you all agree on. Again, it just needs to be communicated from the start.

Lastly, each partner needs to be accountable. Everyone who has "skin in the game" should understand that nobody acts with impunity. For this reason, it is critical to find partners you trust and have faith will make good decisions that are moral, ethical and for the best of the organization and not for any individual. As the company grows and expands and responsibilities become more defined and compartmentalized, knowing you have partners handling important aspects of the business on your behalf will allow you to sleep well at night and free you and your talents to focus on the areas of the business you excel at.

> **Rhett:** Pete and I have always had differing opinions about where capital and resources should be applied. I am more liberal while he is more conservative in regards to the business. Eventually, we met in the middle. Pete is a detail and money guy. He keeps me in line. He says, "Here's your budget and here's what you can spend," and then I go out and I spend twice as much.

> **Pete:** The point is that it is massively important to play off of each other's strengths and weaknesses. That is a true partnership. We knew we had to figure out how we could mesh our skills and values together to work well and get things done. Honestly, I am more calculated when it comes to risk taking, and if Rhett were more like me, it would have taken a very long time to grow the business. On the other hand, if I were more like Rhett, we would have gone bankrupt in the first several months -- maybe even minutes. We would have splurged for expensive office supplies and a kegerator. Okay, I would have supported the kegerator, but the point is we complimented each other. For the records, I'm still using the same office chair I bought seven years ago.

Rhett: It helped that we have the same beliefs and ethics. We both want to do something worthy and significant in our lives that will ultimately help people. You know when someone's heart is in the right place and you can trust him or her. That's what this partnership is about. I trust Pete. I know he will always make the right decisions and look out for our interest and welfare.

GETTING ALONG

When growing a business relationship -- and to a greater extent, a personal one -- you absolutely must learn how to communicate with one another. Much like other personality traits you refine as an entrepreneur, the relationship you have with partners will develop over time, but only if you are open, honest, and frank. Never avoid or postpone conflict and put aside any passive aggressive nature you might have. Allowing a problem or disagreement to fester only makes it more explosive when it finally surfaces.

It is exactly like marriage.

You will spend more time and emotional energy on your business than you will in almost any personal relationship. When things start to go wrong, withdrawing and blaming the other partners only makes matters worse. Instead, be prepared to handle disagreements, disappointments, and frustrations early on and learn to talk about them with each other. In business as in marriage, communication works to reduce tension and help resolution.

At Wild Creations, our opinions and strategic decisions typically converged. We played the "give and take game" to be sure, but we were typically able to negotiate an outcome that we could both live with. Years into our professional partnership, we have been able to avoid major conflicts with one another.

That doesn't mean we haven't had spats. We did, and they were doozies at that.

Pete: I remember a trade show in New York City. We were out for the evening and something came up that rattled our cages. Arguing turned into shouting and Rhett eventually walked out of the bar we had decided on. The next day, we met in the hotel lobby and flagged a cab to the trade show. We sat in the cab like an old married couple after an argument, staring out our windows in complete silence. Neither one of us looked at each other, and we both waited for the other to budge.

Looking back, it is embarrassing to think we acted like that. To this day, I don't even remember what we argued about, but we clearly didn't settle it properly. Luckily, after years of working together, trusting and respecting one another, this disagreement was easy to patch up -- probably over a couple of beers.

Rhett: Essentially, for the last eight years, I've trusted Pete with my life. And, when I'm talking about life, I'm talking about how we feed our families, pay for school, take care of the mortgage -- everything. He was around for the birth of my kids. We are linked by this personal bond, which would never have been possible had it not been for a mutual respect and adoration from starting a business.

Pete: Rhett was with me when I proposed to my wife. He and I were having beers, and I sent her a text. Yeah, I probably shouldn't admit that.

Rhett: That's what this partnership is and what it has been. I don't know what that means for other entrepreneurs or if it helps to take that giant leap or get to the next level. I just know you can't go through the entrepreneurial journey with random people in your life.

> Pete and I have more joint accounts than we do with our wives. Relationships like this don't always work and I understand we are lucky. You must have open communication and talk about everything to make it work. You have to learn how to read each other, feeding off the tone and intonation of the words just like your significant other.
>
> **Pete:** More than dating, a business partnership is like a marriage, with the exception that divorces are much uglier and more expensive. Like a spouse, you should never disrespect or otherwise do anything to undermine your partner. If you're lucky enough to find someone and make it work, then there's no greater recommendation we can make.

History is littered with the carcasses of would-be entrepreneurs who were ripped off or otherwise destroyed by once-trusted partners. Having a partner or partners you trust, respect, and compliment you will infinitely increase the possibility of success.

CHAPTER FIVE

The secret to successful hiring is this: look for the people who want to change the world.

-- Marc Benioff, CEO, Salesforce

BUILDING YOUR TEAM

Entrepreneurship is not a one-person sport, as we emphasized in the last chapter. Beyond business partners, you will need to find managers and employees who are as committed to the business as you -- and who are willing and able to endure the challenges and uncertainty associated with a small company. If you are endeavoring into entrepreneurship directly from a corporate job -- as we did -- you will soon find that finding these people will be infinitely more challenging than you expect.

Regardless, the effort is worth it, as hiring the wrong employees is probably the fastest way to completely derail your company.

The process by which you recruit, screen, hire, and even terminate employees is pretty straightforward. You are in fact bound by many legal guidelines and requirements that dictate how every step in the process is to be carried through. Documenting your hiring process is necessary, as is keeping thorough written records for each employee. The requirements are similar across states, but it is best to consult a professional who is familiar with state and local laws and requirements.

Beyond the process, what is important to point out are your expectations. You may have recruited, interviewed, and hired people in a former job, but hiring people, as a proprietor of a new company is wholly different. Be prepared to set aside any preconceived notion of what it takes to hire and retain employees. More important, make sure your expectations for how your employees will treat you and your business are flexible.

HIRING FOR A NON-TECH STARTUP

When we first hired at Wild Creations, the economy had not had its epic fall. There was plenty of speculation and anxiety, however, and job growth was nonexistent as companies were being very conservative. Add to all of this Wild Creations was headquartered in Myrtle Beach, South Carolina, a relatively small town that was hypersensitive to tourism and business from Memorial Day to Labor Day. The unemployment rate in Myrtle Beach is typically high compared to the rest of the state, but it skyrocketed in the off-season.

With this imbalance in jobs throughout the year, one would think it would be easy to find willing and able bodies seeking gainful year-round employment.

That is what we thought.

The previous owners of Wild Creations operated each summer, from May through September, making and delivering ecosystems to beach and gift stores all along the coast. At the end of the season, like most companies in Myrtle Beach, they would close the office and move back to their home in Canada for the off-season.

Each summer, the family hired back the same two employees. Each off-season, the two employees were released and either found another job or filed for unemployment (as most workers in Myrtle Beach do). When we bought the business, both stayed with us and were happy to learn we were planning on turning the business into a year-round business.

As we started to grow, expand our delivery routes and seek winter retail business, it became apparent we needed to hire more people, specifically delivery drivers and sales associates. The first guy we hired was Pete's landlord at the time, Rodney, who just happened to need a job. He was a fantastic guy with a great personality, incredibly hard working, and ended up working for Wild Creations for almost three years. Unfortunately, because we had such great luck with him as our first hire, our expectations going into our next round of hiring was considerably skewed.

When we decided to bring on another employee, it was the beginning of our first summer in 2007, so we knew the resorts and local restaurants were staffing up for the summer. Again, we figured our opportunity for year-round employment would help us attract aggressive and ambitious talent among the existing pool of people.

We ran an ad in a free online publication, Craigslist, for a delivery driver. In the ad, we asked candidates to drop by the warehouse and complete an application. By the end of the week, we had received almost two hundred applications and felt very confident we could find at least one person to fill the position.

We split the stack of applications and each took half to review. By the time we were done, we each had found zero applicants who met the strict criteria we had. Granted, we had high standards, but we were shocked that we could not find one candidate we could both agree was worthy of hiring.

Again, we had over two hundred applicants.

We went back to the stacks a second time with lower expectations. We began looking for applications with applicable experience and achievements -- many applied with unrelated or no experience.

We looked for candidates with an education or pertinent training -- many had little to none.

By the time we were done, our criteria were mainly: 1) legible handwriting and 2) minimal spelling errors.

We did eventually find a candidate we both liked. He answered our call and visited the warehouse for an interview. We wanted our new driver to hit the road right away for a trade show to see the product in action and learn the selling process first hand. He was incredibly excited, as were we, so we shook hands, had him complete the applicable paperwork, and planned on meeting Thursday morning to depart for the show.

He never showed up for the job. No call. No email. Just no show.

Disappointed and let down, we went through our stack again and found another reasonable applicant. As with the previous candidate, he visited the office, interviewed with us, shook hands, filled out paperwork, and parted ways with plans to meet the coming Thursday for a trade show.

Again, he never showed. No call. No email. Just no show.

Through that second round of hiring, we met with new eight new candidates, shook hands, completed paperwork, and parted ways with plans to meet for a trade show or delivery run. And eight times, our candidate did not show up. It was comical and definitely tapered our expectations for what to expect for future hiring.

THE STRATEGY SESSION

That first summer past without ever hiring a second delivery driver. We did, however, end up hiring a sales manager and a warehouse manager. We hired them at the end of the summer, which proved to be infinitely easier to do with the glut of people out of jobs for the off-season.

We worked every day of the week that summer, often driving day after day without seeing the apartment we shared, and by the Fall realized that we had not implemented any of the strategic planning we had done hundreds of times for the small businesses as business consultants. We had fallen into the entrepreneurial trap: too busy working in the business to work on it.

With five employees now, we decided to pull the team together for a strategic action planning session, to debrief about the summer and to plan for the future, and ultimately provide a little inspiration to everyone going into the fourth quarter.

> **Rhett:** We would typically do a strategy meeting with a client in a conference room of some sort, but we didn't have that kind of space in our warehouse. So, we ended up renting a hotel room on the beach, which was incredibly cheap in the off-season and about the only space we could afford. We had a team of five employees, and they all sat around the dining room table full of anxiety. They were a good crew. A motley one, but a good crew, nonetheless. Pete and I wanted to get everyone together to have this action-planning meeting as a team building exercise. I was all about getting their feedback, listening to their ideas, and concerns, and then getting their buy-in to the vision and goals of the company.
>
> It was soon clear that none of our new employees had ever sat down with their employers to come up with an overall game plan for the business, much less a vision. No one had ever asked for their feedback or their opinions. As we went on, the meeting started to spiral into arguments and misgivings. The discussion turned from action-oriented goals for increasing sales to blame for stealing other's lunch from the refrigerator and failure to clean the bathroom. Everyone was talking over each other, and we were getting nowhere fast.
>
> Finally, I went over to the whiteboard we had dragged along, snagged a smelly marker, and simply wrote three words:

ONE MILLION FROGS

The meeting stopped as I wrote this, and everyone stared. It was tough to read their expressions, but there were clearly some smirks and questionable looks. They sat staring back at me with glassy eyes, and I realized they just didn't get it.

Pete: Rhett wrote the expression as a vision statement, meaning we as a company, as a team, we're going to set our sights on selling one million frogs. It was the type of vision statement we would work toward with our clients. The type I learned about in business school. It was ambitious and bold, and it was meant to draw everyone into a common cause.

After the shell-shock wore off, the team in the room laughed, joked and even got a little belligerent about the idea of selling one million frogs. Up to that time, we were on pace to sell twenty thousand that year. They kept calling out "impossible" and "how the fuck are we going to do that?"

I immediately understood the impact and what this vision meant. We had been trying to come up with a company mantra around which we could all rally. I looked around the room and tried to pull everyone in, saying as encouragingly as I could, "Listen, we need a vision. Something to shoot for. We can do this, guys! What do you say?"

I realized quickly that not everyone was on the same level. Everyone had different life experiences and priorities. Helping us reach one million frogs was not one of their priorities. Making it to the next paycheck was way more important. It was an eye-opening business life lesson. We had compiled a team that was nowhere near ready for the grand plans we had.

Needless to say, that strategy session did not last long, and it was a very long time before we held another.

In the end, our employees were not concerned about the acronyms, business school definitions, or complex consulting strategy sessions. They were not familiar with spreadsheets or business plans or matrices. They were interested only in getting paid for the work they did today. If we could not provide this for them, then they would move on and find someone who would. They had zero interest in our goal of building a legacy business. And while we did not necessarily believe that everyone would be, it was greatly disappointing to find that we could not get them motivated to a common cause.

> **Rhett:** We were coming from serious professional jobs and had been hiring people with masters and doctorate degrees. Now, we were getting applicants who didn't even have a resume or would come into the interview in T-shirts and shorts. I had to change my expectations of people and what they wanted out of the job and us, and then reassess what their motivations might be. At one point, we stopped asking for resumes and started qualifying people by the lack of (or at least limited) criminal record.

ADVENTURES IN HIRING

To say we had a few employee misfires would be an enormous understatement. Even though our expectations were properly adjusted after the first summer debacle of eight failed delivery driver hires, nothing could prepare us for the series of disastrous employee choices that followed.

Miami and bust: Hire only the best.

When starting Wild Creations, we agreed on the need to hire the right people. Unfortunately, emotions and empathy often influence hiring, at least until a bad experience bites you. This happened to us with one of our first hires.

For sake of anonymity, we will call this early hire Trey. Trey was actually one of the eight delivery drivers we hired who failed to show for his first day of work without the courtesy of a phone call. When the first summer ended, Trey called again and explained he had a significant personal issue come up, which kept him from coming the morning he was to start. He explained he was too embarrassed to call and felt he lost his chance. He went on to explain how much he liked the business and us, and he wanted a second chance.

Trey was a thirty-something New Englander who seemed to be a good guy. Pete liked him and felt he had the enthusiasm and zeal to be a good sales representative. They agreed over the phone to meet up on Monday morning and get rolling.

Monday rolled around, and again, no Trey.

A few days later, Trey called again and explained that on the morning we were to meet, he had car problems and his mother had fallen ill.

On a side note, we felt bad for the families of most of our early hires, as it always seemed at least one family member would fall ill or die at some point in their employment with Wild Creations.

Against our better judgment, but because he was completely apologetic and almost begging for a third chance, we decided to give Trey one more try. He actually did show up for our next meeting, and he worked out for a couple of weeks. After a few sales and delivery trips with Rhett, we decided to let him do a delivery on his own. We loaded one of our extended cab, white cargo vans full of frogs and sent Trey to Miami to meet a client. All seemed great, and we were feeling like Trey was really going to work out.

A few days later, we received a call from Trey. Something had come up, and he could not make the delivery. In fact, he quit on the spot. We asked him about the van and the merchandise, to which he replied, “It’s in Miami.”

He gave us directions to the van, and Rhett drove down to pick it up -- 10 hours away.

Needless to say, Trey was a learning lesson. As entrepreneurs, we had always believed in supporting and believing in the general good nature of others. Trey killed that just a little, but more important, he refined and solidified our understanding of good hires.

As entrepreneurs, it is generally in our good nature to want to believe in others and give opportunities to succeed. The number one priority, however, should be to find the right people for a job. If you feel guilty about this, consider the fact that bad employees can be toxic, which affect everyone in the organization. You owe it to your other employees and stakeholders to choose only the best people for your business.

Stranded in Ohio: Go with your gut.

Trey had all the warning signs of a bad employee. After failing to show or call for two straight appointments, we should have known better than to give him a third chance. In addition to being persistent, however, Trey was convincing in a used car salesman manner. When you meet employees who talk the talk, tread cautiously, as we learned the hard way.

Another early hire, we will call him Ramirez, was another thirty-something from the northeast. Like Trey, he was incredibly enthusiastic and ambitious, and he made a convincing argument as to why he wanted to be part of our startup. Unfortunately, he could not provide any references, which should have been a red flag.

After some careful consideration, we again decided to give him a chance. At the time, we were entering our first winter, in 2007, and this was the first time that the company had attempted to do business in the cold, winter months, so we were in uncharted territory. In order to make it to the Christmas holiday, which we were fairly certain would be lucrative and successful, we had to make it through the slow months of fall. One way to generate money during this time was to attend "cash and carry" trade shows, such as boat and gun shows in small town convention centers. These trade shows allowed us to sell merchandise at the shows, and to keep the business open. We were attending six to eight every month.

In November, we had a string of large trade shows over two weeks that promised to be very profitable. The first weekend was in Ohio and Illinois, and the second weekend was in Pennsylvania and New York. Because of the distances, we loaded two vans full of enough merchandise to cover two shows each. Rodney and Rhett headed to Illinois while Ramirez and his teenage son headed to Ohio.

Unfortunately, there was a heavy snowstorm in Ohio that weekend, and the show was a terrible failure. We had almost no revenue, and with the cost of registration, hotel, food, and incidentals, it was a significant loss. After the show, early the next week, Ramirez phoned Pete, who was still in Myrtle Beach managing the office, and told him he did not want the job any more. Additionally, he had no money to get home and asked Pete to wire him money for gas and lodging to return home.

This was a huge blow, as missing the next show would have been devastating to the business.

> **Pete:** This was not good news. We already took a bath on the Ohio show, so missing the next show in Chicago would have killed our cash flow. What's more, we had a van full of merchandise that was useless in Myrtle Beach. More than likely, we would have had to scrap the entire lot of aquariums.
>
> I phoned Rhett, who was finishing a show in New York with Rodney, and told him Ramirez had quit. I needed to get to the

van and go to the show, but we had to keep Ramirez in Ohio until I could get there. Rhett told me to call Ramirez back and tell him to stay put, and that he would call me back in a couple of hours.

I called and convinced Ramirez to stay at his hotel until I called him back, and he agreed. Several hours passed. It then turned very strange.

I received a frantic call from Ramirez, who was panicked and shouting on the phone that Rhett had arrived at the hotel, pulled a gun on him, took the van, and left him and his son in the middle of the street in the snow. He had no money to get a hotel or pay for a ride back home. He was desperate, on the verge of tears, and begging me to wire him just enough money to get back.

I hung up, called Rhett, but could not reach him. I tried a few more times in the hour that followed, but eventually I wired Ramirez his pay for the time he had spent on the road.

When Rhett finally called me back, the real story came out.

Rhett: When I got Pete's call, Rodney and I drove straight to Ohio to meet Ramirez. We arrived at his hotel about six or seven hours later. I asked him for the keys to the van, which he refused to, give me until I gave him a thousand dollars. He knew I had it from the show we were coming from, and he essentially held the keys hostage. Since I knew he still had the petty cash from the show, I refused to give him any more money.

Regardless, I was angry he was leaving us in a bad situation by quitting in the middle of the week.

I was able to convince him to hand over the keys, and as soon as I had them, I split and told him to get a bus ticket home with the money from the petty cash he still had. I jumped in the van,

> Rodney jumped in his, and we started to leave. Ramirez ran out into the street and lay down in front of the van and started screaming that we were going to run over and kill him.
>
> The police arrived shortly thereafter, lights ablaze, and Ramirez just went nuts. He insisted Rodney had threatened him with a gun, and we were trying to run him over. Rodney did keep legally concealed weapon with him, and once he and the officers chatted cordially, the police allowed us to leave.
>
> I had no idea he had called Pete and asked him for money, but he had plenty with the petty cash we left behind, not to mention the damage he caused to our merchandise and the time and resources we wasted driving to him. Rodney and I ended splitting up and attending the other two shows on our own.

The experience with Ramirez did not end on that snowy highway in Ohio. A few weeks after the incident, Ramirez sent us a letter demanding ten thousand dollars, else he would slander us and take Wild Creations to court. Of course, we did not pay, and instead reported the extortion attempt to the police, who used the signed letter as evidence to issue a restraining order.

Ramirez was a great salesman. He had convinced us early that he could be a huge asset to the business, but we failed to recognize the warning signs, namely that he had a speckled past and no references. As well, we both just did not feel right about him. Our guts told us to be cautious, but his enthusiasm was difficult to overlook.

It is easy for entrepreneurs to get caught up in enthusiastic sales pitches, but always go with your gut when you hire.

Kiosk lessons: Be prepared for anything

We could write an entire book about the hiring follies of Wild Creations. Indeed, I think we saw just about everything. The overwhelming lesson for others is you cannot predict the behavior employees. You can motivate and compensate them, include them in business planning, but in the end, be prepared for anything.

No experience proved this more than our experience running mall kiosks during our first winter in business, in 2007.

That year, we ran ten retail mall kiosks in shopping malls (the carts located in the center walking paths) in North Carolina, South Carolina, Georgia, and Florida. We hired able-bodied employees to work the kiosk while we drove and delivered merchandise throughout the week.

The first year in retail proved to be much more of a headache than it was worth. For starters, when an employee decided not to show up for work, which happened more often than we can remember, one of us had to detour from our delivery route to drive to the mall with the missing clerk and spend a week opening and running the kiosk while interviewing, hiring, and training a new clerk.

One Sunday afternoon, we received a call from the general manager of a mall in Charlotte, North Carolina, who informed us the police were at our kiosk arresting our manager for "assault and battery." It turned out she had a misgiving with a passing patron, an argument ensued, and our manager kicked the patron down a set of stairs near the kiosk. Luckily, nobody was seriously hurt.

Kiosk employee mishaps happened all winter that year.

We received emailed pictures from customers of our kiosk representative unabashedly sleeping in the chair during prime shopping hours -- twice.

We received receiving phone calls from customers standing at our unattended kiosk, using the kiosk phone, and asking how they could purchase an EcoAquarium -- all while our rep claimed to be working.

At least we had honest and helpful customers.

We had employees who refused to sell, employees who took money from the register, and employees who neglected the product.

Maybe the most frustrating (even more than employees getting arrested) were the employees who called to ask ridiculously simple questions, which we called "hair on fire" questions. They typically went like this:

Employee: "Hey, I was wondering, my head is on fire, and I can't figure out what to do about it. What should I do?"

Us: "Put the fire out."

Employee: "Brilliant. Thanks."

That is not to say we are being insensitive, but when you receive those calls as the proprietor of the business, you cannot help but wonder what else is and is not getting done that you don't know about.

It keeps you awake at night.

Manager challenges: Do not promote out of desperation

With the problems we had in hiring employees, you can imagine how difficult it was to find managers. Like hiring, promoting people to positions of authority and responsibility requires a good deal of diligence and planning. Starting ten kiosks and being on the road week after week required us to find people to manage other aspects of the business. We ended up promoting prematurely -- or maybe more aptly, out of desperate need -- and it ended up hurting us.

Our first sales manager, a guy we will call Jimmy, was a large and imposing personality who had all of the characteristics and charm of a southern car salesman. He was affable, enthusiastic, and had a well-dressed dapper flair about him. After working with him for a few weeks, we decided to put him in charge of the kiosks in North and South Carolina while we managed the kiosks further south. Although he looked the part of a wealthy salesperson, he never had money, so we made the decision to have a company credit card issued in his name in order to help him manage the kiosks from the road.

One morning, while reconciling the credit card activity, we noticed Jimmy's card had reached its maximum balance -- about fifteen hundred dollars -- just a couple of days after paying it down. More concerning was the fact that a number of charges, 1200 hundred dollars total, were from a "gentlemen's club" in North Carolina.

We immediately contact Jimmy who embarrassingly and somewhat indignantly confirmed the charges, and assured us they were "team building" activities with "his employees."

Needless to say, one of us was in a van driving to North Carolina that day to replace him.

The other significant issue we had was with our warehouse manager. Because we were on the road all the time, we decided to "promote" a warehouse employee to manager status to oversee the operations.

We chose an employee, whom we'll call AJ, mostly because she was the oldest and seemingly most mature of the group. Not a good criteria to go by, considering she did not have the experience and, more important, we suspected she might have a drug problem. Given the group we had, however, she was our best candidate.

Again, we promoted out of desperation, which is never a good thing.

AJ actually lasted a while and was a decent employee. She had personality conflicts with a few of her co-workers requiring intervention, but when she was not stepping on toes, she kept the warehouse operating.

The real problem came when we took AJ on a road trip to attend a trade show. We wanted to cross-train employees and provide our warehouse staff the opportunity to see the sales side of the business. This is a great strategy for employees, but with AJ, it turned out to be a disaster. After getting lost in New Jersey, she and her travel partner, our office manager at the time, pulled over to get directions. AJ panicked and ended up taking three hundred dollars from the petty cash and splitting, never to be heard from again. It was a very strange event, and one that left our office manager alone in a large city to run a trade show on her own.

Again, we were lucky the event did not turn out worse.

Sabotage: Too good to be true

In the spring of our breakout year, 2009, we went on a major hiring spree. Our staff grew from ten to fifty in a few weeks as we geared up for our new account and transition into the toy industry. We were growing so fast, we literally hired people off the streets.

One such hire, a young and energetic guy we'll call Kevin, arrived with resume in hand and enthusiasm in his step. We hired him on the spot and started training him in our warehouse. On a couple of occasions, we took him on deliveries and started to groom him to meet clients.

Kevin was professional, asked the right questions, and showed incredible promise as an employee.

He was almost too good of an employee.

By fall of that year, Kevin was at the forefront of our discussions about new managers. One day, however, he phoned our warehouse manager and apologetically resigned due to a family issue that required his immediate attention. We accepted his resignation, but we were emphasized that had a job if and when he ever returned. That was the last we saw Kevin.

It was not the last time we heard from him.

A few weeks later, around Thanksgiving, an online video surfaced from People for the Ethical Treatment of Animals (PETA). It turned out Kevin was an undercover “agent” for PETA, secretly filming the operations and manipulating the video to appear as if we were harming our frogs. After the video, the police arrived to inspect our property, and we fielded a few phone calls about the video. It all turned out fine, as we were never harming the frogs and indeed were very transparent about our operations.

While we had numerous battles with PETA over the years (explained in a later chapter), Kevin took a bit of spark out of our step. It started to feel like we could not trust anyone. In hindsight, even Kevin had warning signs. He had no local address and was actually from the same city where PETA had its headquarters. When we were on the road together, Kevin would often hunker down under his bed sheets with his laptop, though we never suspected anything.

If nothing else, the experience again taught us to be diligent about our hiring and never take an employee for granted.

As with any entrepreneurial experience, bad employee encounters are par for the course. Handling them requires patience and experience, though having the right expectations ahead of time helps. Starting with good hiring practices is a great start to finding the right people for your team.

MOTIVATING AND MANAGING EMPLOYEES

A great many of the employee horror stories we have had are due to bad hiring decisions. We did the best we could with the pool of talent available, and Wild Creations was disadvantaged as a startup company with limited resources, trying to grow during one of the worst recessions of a generation. We had neither the financial capabilities to pay large salaries and offer benefits. We were trying to find employees who could see the long-term potential of Wild Creations and our vision, and who might be willing to work long hours for little pay to be part of the future.

We were willing to do it, so how could it be so difficult to find others?

It turns out most people do not want to work for free. Most cannot. And we found a direct correlation between the wages of our employees and managers and the rate at which they quit. When we decided to pay a little more for someone we felt was qualified for a position, that individual usually stayed for a while, and vice versa.

Also, the type of employees we were attracting had completely different goals. Pay trumped everything. For instance, when we did offer an employee-sponsored health insurance package very early, almost every employee opted out, preferring instead to have the additional money rather than insurance.

Regardless of how bold and ambitious your entrepreneurial plans might be, do not expect to hire an entire team right away who is willing to sleep on the floor and eat bread and jam for weeks on end while you grow the business. You will need to find other ways to incentivize them.

Another important aspect of managing employees you need to keep in mind is shedding the bad ones. There are always employees who hate to work in organizations -- or to work in general -- and will loathe their job and, more than likely, you as the proprietor, regardless of any benefit or compensation you offer.

Some employees are just course and rough around the edges. In one incident, we had a gentlemen come to our office asking, “This ain’t one of those $5.25 an hour jobs, is it?” to which we replied, “No sir, the minimum wage is $7.25, and thank you for stopping by.”

Other times, you have employees who will unabashedly try to work the systems. On numerous occasions, we interviewed people who asked to be paid “under the table” or through a spouse in order to keep their unemployment or disability benefits. Of course, we never agreed, and for the most part, we would end the interview abruptly at just the suggestion.

Employees who demonstrate the willingness to cheat the system or prioritize pay and small details (“Do I have to be here at 9:00 a.m.?”) are the types of employees you need to avoid. Not only will they become a concern in your organization, they often tend to be toxic to other employees, spewing negativity among the team.

With that said, you need to do everything to “keep the keepers.” Although we have shared employee horror stories, it is worth noting we have found great employees as well. Entrepreneurs need to hold on to the good employees when you find them. And while a great employee does not necessarily imply an employee willing to work for near nothing to support your vision, keep in mind a decent paycheck is not always the primary motivation for all employees.

When you find a keeper, take time to understand his or her personal and professional goals and ambitions in order to determine the best way to compensate and motivate them.

If you haven’t already studied it, it is worth knowing and understanding the “Maslow Hierarchy of Needs.” Developed by one of the pioneers of modern psychology, Dr. Abraham Maslow, the hierarchy puts forth a structure for understanding the general needs of all people as follows:

1. **Physiological**: breathing, water, food, sleep, sex, homeostasis, excretion

2. **Safety**: security of body, employment, resources, morality, family, health, property

3. **Love/Belonging**: friendship, family, sexual intimacy

4. **Esteem**: self-esteem, confidence, achievement, respect of others, respect by others

5. **Self Actualization**: morality, creativity, spontaneity, problem solving, lack of prejudice, acceptance of facts

The needs and desires of each individual fall somewhere in this range.

For those who find themselves at the bottom (Physiological), primary needs for survival are the priority. Food, water, and shelter. As you move through the hierarchy, reaching the top (Self Actualization), individuals seek more than money and survival; they drive to achieve personal and peer acceptance and respect and ultimately to reach his or her full potential.

Understanding where your employee's fall into this mix is important. For employees who are trying to reach self-actualization, the promise of a decent paycheck and two weeks of vacation is not as important as the opportunity to gain valuable experience and to move up in the organization. On the opposite end, the potential of a promotion or a partnership does not pay the bills or put food on the table.

Lastly, remember it is fine and actually preferable to have people who fall into all levels of Maslow's Hierarchy. An organization full of self-actualization types, typically aggressive and overly ambitious, will cause issues with the delegation of responsibilities. You need people in the organization who are productive and enjoy the security and minimal challenge of regular job duties. Find and nurture the balance in your organization.

LEAD BY EXAMPLE

Without a doubt, leadership skills are the most important thing you can offer your employees. Putting forth a positive and enthusiastic attitude is critical, especially through troubled times and business challenges. While it is understandable that not all entrepreneurs are "built" the same and may have difficulty leading a new organization, especially if it is your first, remember leadership skills are organic and can be learned and refined with experience. Below are just a few of personality traits entrepreneurs need to lead their employees.

1. **Be positive and enthusiastic.** Employees bring their own personal issues and problems, so they do not need to be inundated with the issues and problems of the business. Handle them with tact and remember the old saying, "shit flows uphill," and you are at the river's depository.

2. **Be responsible.** Remember your employees depend on you for their livelihood, so treat that responsibility with respect. Do not expect them to make personal sacrifices for your organization.

3. **Be authentic.** It is very difficult to get behind someone if their ambitions and cause seem fake. Be honest and transparent with your employees, and give them a real reason to support you.

4. **Be clear.** Communicate your expectations and the company's goals, plans and policies. Employees need to understand the mission and feel good about helping to accomplish that mission.

5. **Be generous.** Employees will always appreciate a bonus or pay increase, but they will also appreciate generosity in other ways. Dishing credit and appreciation to employees and demonstrating their value to the organization will make employees feel meaningful and significant.

6. **Be an example.** You should never ask anything of your staff you would not ask of yourself. Employees are more likely to work hard for an organization or someone they feel works hard for them. Your employees may not love you, but they will respect your integrity and work ethic.

7. **Celebrate often.** Communicate good news with the team. Nothing will make them feel more valuable than if their daily grind is recognized through the achievements of the business.

Every employee is going to react to your leadership in different ways, because each has their own set of expectations and ambitions. Also, every person you hire is going to bring different skills and experiences to your organization. Interview well and get to know them. Tailor your approach accordingly to assure you are balancing the needs of the team and the organization.

When we started Wild Creations, we tried to impart the leadership skills we had learned and refined after years of working in corporate America and the international consulting world. We were wrong. Our initial set of employees had completely different goals and priorities than growing our small startup fledgling of a company. Getting them to see our vision for the company was not just difficult, it proved to be impossible. It came down to job security and a steady paycheck, which as a startup was difficult to provide. In the end, we were able to find a set of key employees who grew with the company, and when times got tough and we downsized the organization, we kept as many as we could. To some degree, we kept more than we needed.

That is just what you do.

FINDING EMPLOYEES

If we have not made it clear with the stories we have told in this chapter, finding the right employees is crucial. Finding the right employees involves interviewing properly and avoiding certain pitfalls. You need to start with the search, however, and where you look for employees can prove to be just as important as every other step.

You first need to identify the skills and character traits you need, or more appropriately the holes in the business that you need to fill. Placing free online ads or simply hiring someone off the street is usually not the most effective way to find the skill sets your business needs.

Whatever you do, avoid hiring out despairingly, even if you have an overwhelming immediate need. When you do hire out of desperation, you may find yourself with an employee who leaves a van full of merchandise and keys ten hours away.

The old adage "who you know is more important than what you know" is very applicable, especially now that you are on the business ownership side of the desk. Referrals from advisors, colleagues, friends, and social contacts can be a productive and very effective way of finding the help you need. You do, however, need to have fair and legal application and hiring practices to assure someone you pass up for a job does not have grounds to pursue legal action. Carefully review the federal hiring guidelines and be sure to implement them into your company policies.

And while it may seem a good idea, be very cautious when considering friends and family as potential employees. As dear as they are, and as willing as they may be to "help" you as you start and grow the business, very few personal relationship ever make the professional transition without ending very badly.

In the end, it is worth the expense to place ads in reputable publications for jobs, open accounts with reputable websites, and ask around for referrals. For important managerial hires, focus on industry or professional publications where your candidates will be looking. Establish a strong network with other professionals in your area and industry who will field a call and inquiry about potential candidates. Again, be sure to screen your candidates, ask thought-provoking interview questions, and check references and backgrounds before hiring.

If you have any questions or reservations, settle them before you make a decision. Entering a relationship with an employee with reservations sets a shaky stage to start.

Another option entrepreneurs should consider is outsourcing tasks to consultants, freelancers, or temporary services before making permanent staff hires. Outsourcing provides you a wide range of options from which to choose and can ultimately save you money by avoiding employment taxes and benefits. Outsourcing can also bring in skills necessary for temporary projects and jobs; those that once completed would no longer require a full time employee. Some tasks in fact should be outsourced, at least from the start. Legal counsel, accounting, and even administrative assistants can be relatively inexpensive and readily available online now.

Through crowdsourcing websites, you can screen and hire people online to do specific tasks on a freelance basis, such as graphic artists, copywriters, editors, web designers, database programmers, business consultants, translators, and marketing specialists. Contractors with these sites have portfolios and resumes posted in their profiles, as well as ratings from other clients who have used their services. They will submit bids on your projects, along with detailed proposals as to how they plan to do it and how they expect to be paid. Remember that it is not always best to select the lowest bidder, as you often get what you pay for. Be thorough and review the proposals. When possible, interview prospective contractors by phone or email prior to hiring and confirm credentials through third party verification agencies.

As we discovered, painfully at times, you may not always end up with the greatest pool of potential hires from which to choose, choosing the "best of the worse" will do your business more harm than good. Always set a goal to get the right people on your team.

CHAPTER SIX

Always deliver more than expected.

-- Larry Page, Co-Founder, Google

GROWING YOUR BUSINESS

Few new businesses start making heaps of money right out of the gate. Most, in fact, fail. Getting into business to get wealthy, therefore, should not be your primary objective.

With that said, understand a business that isn't moving forward is moving backwards. Yes, you might be happy just maintaining the same level of income from year to year, as long as it meets your needs and pays the bills, but if you have demonstrated the courage to endeavor into entrepreneurship -- and have had the fortune to find success at doing so -- you would be doing yourself a disservice by not considering how to grow your business.

Business building is part of entrepreneurial thinking. In the dynamic marketplace, change is constant and today is often instant. You have to keep your finger on the pulse of business, always looking for new ways to expand and improve your business, else risk becoming completely obsolete.

Our original business strategy -- the business investment and holdings company -- clearly did not include frogs or mall kiosks and trade shows. That changed, of course, when Lehman

Brothers filed bankruptcy and we were left holding a small, retail Frog Company.

As the economy continued to linger, we did eventually accept our fate and embrace Wild Creations (and frogs) as our destiny. When that reality set in, we set off to do whatever we could to make the company survive this turbulent and uncertain time.

One strategy we embarked on was to attend every consumer trade show and fair we could. With no money for marketing, it was the best way to drive revenue and cash flow while also getting our frogs and our company out there.

During the first two years, we were attending two to three shows every week in almost every conceivable city and convention center along the east coast. This required each of us to drive, set up and work the booth, and do everything in our power to push sales. We went to every show that would allow us to participate, including pet shows, toy shows, and even boat and gun shows.

Anything to create visibility for the frogs.

It was in fact the annual Toy Industry Association (TIA) Toy Fair in New York City, the largest in the western hemisphere, that got Wild Creations into the toy industry. It was February 2009, and up until that time, we had always targeted the toy industry for the EcoAquarium, but just had not found the "in" we needed to get our foot in the door.

Late in 2008, we had started shipping EcoAquariums to a toy store in Nebraska, who could not keep the product on her shelf. The store was selling out sixty to seventy a week, and the owner loved us. As a board member for the American Specialty Toy Retailing Association (ASTRA), an association that included every small specialty toy store in the nation, she began singing praises publicly about our company. She strongly encouraged us to attend TIA Toy Fair in New York City.

It was by far the largest toy fair, and consequently the most expensive and risky, that we had considered.

> **Pete:** We almost didn't go to the event because registration is very expensive and it was held in Manhattan. We didn't have the money to cover that. Regardless, we eventually decided to take the risk.
>
> We registered late, which meant we got poor placement in the massive Javits Convention Center. We could not afford to stay in Manhattan, so we stayed in New Jersey. We couldn't even afford parking, so we took the bus to the Port Authority and then took a cab.
>
> The whole thing was a huge cost and risk, one in which we did not have the funds for, but we figured it out and made it happen.
>
> **Rhett:** We loaded up the vans in Myrtle Beach and headed to New York. We stayed at the Econo-Lodge across the river in Secaucus, New Jersey. We ate cheap and shared a cramped hotel room. We did what it took to get it done.

During that show, we hoped to secure twenty to thirty new clients who would help pay for the show and create some income in perpetuity. More important, we wanted publicity for the EcoAquarium and Wild Creations.

When we arrived at our booth, in what felt like the sub-basement of the Javits Center, it was tiny and far off the beaten path. We wondered if we had made a big mistake.

On day one, our concerns were quelled, as we had over a hundred clients walk up to the booth and commit to an order by handing over a business card and saying, "Send me a case." For an industry trade show, this is extremely rare, and we owed much of that success to the relationship we had with our good friend who owned the toy store in Nebraska.

The attention from the small specialty store owners was fantastic, but as that first day progressed, we slowly came to realize that we now had a big problem on our hand.

We did not have a "case pack." In fact, we were not even approved to ship live frogs. At that time, we were sending small shipments of EcoAquariums through a major delivery carrier without permission. Now, we had hundreds of stores that wanted frogs.

Of course, this is the dream problem for an entrepreneur.

> **Pete:** The second day at the show was just as crazy busy. I had to call in a friend from the area to help at the booth, handing out business cards and brochures. Several big companies, such as Toys-R-Us, hearing of the buzz stopped by and inquired how to get the frogs on their shelves. Countless toy reps also visited asking to represent us. It was overwhelming but awesome. And the entire time, we had to fake that we were ready to ship when, in fact, we could not.

> **Rhett:** We had to turn away all of the big retailers because we had no way to distribute through their complicated distribution centers. More important, we did not want to commit and then have to turn them down, so we were honest and forthcoming. Of course, we took everybody's business card and initiated many great relationships. Then, Brookstone came by, and they would not take no for an answer.

When the toy rep from Brookstone came by, we were just as honest with him as we were with the other big retailers. Regardless, he invited us to visit him and his associates at their headquarters in New Hampshire at the conclusion the trade show. We were incredulous, wondering how a store that sells vibrating chairs and mattresses wanted a frog aquarium.

Indulging in our curiosity and surprising success from the show, we drove to the Brookstone office immediately after the show with a couple of EcoAquariums we had left. We arrived at their gorgeous office building at the end of 1 Brookstone Way and were immediately enthralled with the glass-encased lobby. As a fresh new crystal-white snow fell outside, the receptionist escorted us to a spacious conference room. We settled in and placed our single EcoAquarium frog habitat in the center of the table. We had no idea what to expect.

After a few minutes, the toy buyer we met walked in with another formal looking fellow who turned out to be the vice president of sales. Over the next hour, several people filed in and out of the conference room, from the web designer to product designer to the individual in charge of copyrights. Each stopped and examined the EcoAquarium, often rubbing their chin and saying things like "this is great" and "when can we get it?"

Although we were overcome with excitement, we were a bit nervous at the idea of getting a deal with Brookstone. They wanted it, and it was apparent they wanted it badly.

How in the hell would we get it to them?

> **Pete:** After the parade of buyers and product designers filed out, the Brookstone rep and the vice president of sales and marketing wanted to talk business. As they started asking questions, I remember feeling like I was caught in a tunnel, with thousands of question in my own mind. They asked if we could ship to a distribution center, and before I could chime in to say "eventually", Rhett answered "yes." I didn't contradict him, because to a certain extent, he was right. We could -- I just wasn't sure how yet.
>
> The next topic was price. Of course, we knew how much the frog aquarium cost, but we had no idea how much it would cost to package, ship and service the account. I remember Rhett and I were on one side of the table, with my laptop open, tapping a few numbers on an empty spreadsheet that the Brookstone team couldn't see. I typed, "I have no idea" on

the sheet, and we both looked at it and nodded approvingly. I then offered a price.

We went back and forth for a few minutes, but finally agreed on a price that made them happy and that, at least then, I felt we could work around. That thirteen-hour drive back to Myrtle Beach was quiet, as we both pondered the task ahead of us in silence.

Rhett: I knew this was our shot and we had to take it. Frankly, I was tired of driving those damn frogs all over the place. If we could figure out how to ship them, then hallelujah! I knew we would figure out that detail -- I wasn't worried about it at all. If it failed, then so be it. It wouldn't be our first failure.

Actually, I wasn't so much confident as desperate, and I knew we needed to give it a shot. I had to feel, believe, think, and act like we could. I knew we could figure it out.

When we arrived in Myrtle Beach from the visit to Brookstone in New Hampshire, we got to work immediately. It was actually nice to be working on the business instead of being trapped working in it. We contacted our rep at FedEx and over the next few days received our live animal-shipping certificate. It helped that we were already shipping and knew what was needed -- we did not tell them this, of course. It also helped that we had a great FedEx rep that supported our company and our effort. The support turned out great for her, as Wild Creations was her largest account at our peak and became the largest exporter out of Myrtle Beach for a while.

We also had another problem. Brookstone was projecting significant sales, easily twenty times more than what we were used to. To prepare for the demand, we expanded our warehouse by leasing four spaces adjacent to ours (including Bubba's shop, which had recently become vacant), purchasing new equipment and hiring like crazy. Our biggest problem, however, was inventory. We barely had enough money to expand the business, much less buy all the necessary inventory that was required to meet Brookstone's projections. Moreover, with ordering and shipping, and Brookstone's 60 to 90 payment terms, we were looking at inventory carrying costs lasting six to eight months.

To cover this, we communicated with our vendors and, through a great deal of cajoling, were able to convince most of them to carry the costs themselves. It was a risky endeavor for them -- made only slightly easier to swallow with the Brookstone commitments we had -- but because we had spent the previous two years working closely with them, constantly staying in touch and working through our growing pains, we had their trust. By the time we were ready to ship, we had all stakeholders in our business on board.

The relationships we had with our vendors is an important lesson for other entrepreneurs. Establishing trust early in your business -- or more precisely, avoiding actions that destroy your trust -- is crucial when growing your company. Shared risk is easier to ask for when you have proven your word and not burned bridges. Of course, it helps having a commitment from a large retailer.

A more important lesson is taking the risk altogether. For starters, had we not attended Toy Fair in 2009, we would never have meet Brookstone nor reached the hundreds of clients that resulted from attending. Looking back, we never really questioned attending, as we had attended numerous trade shows to that point and to a great degree were confident we would be successful enough to at least break even. With that said, when we finally had the opportunity in front of Brookstone, knowing full well that we had no right to be sitting there, we took our chance.

That is what entrepreneurs do. They take the risk and never look back.

LEVERAGING TRADE SHOWS

Trade shows are an important part of any business. Some may

argue that trade shows are obsolete or not nearly as cost effective for marketing purposes, but done properly, they can be great for generating revenue and increasing visibility.

We have a love-hate relationship with trade shows, because for all of their benefits, they are also an incredible pain in the ass. Travel time, set up and break down time, countless hours of talking, dried parched lips, sore throats and aching backs and feet are enough to dissuade anyone from partaking. And of course there is the uncertainty and stress.

Once you get past that, however, you find you make incredible relationships with other vendors, see interesting places, and learn that as ugly as they are, Crocs are amazing shoes. Also, if done properly, you can find trade shows incredibly lucrative for the business.

It goes without saying you should have an attractive display, but when you are starting out that may not be possible. Most small businesses at trade shows rely on a table with a drape (more of a dining room table cover) and a banner that hangs on the back wall. This set up is fine, because a good sales pitch can help make even the most modest display stand out. It's about you.

A checklist is important, as we have on more than one occasion forgotten something important, like business cards or sales brochures. And nothing will kill your budget (and your mood) faster than having to find a local print shop and rush order printed materials that you left on your desk back in the office.

Above all, a successful trade show comes down to hustle. We were always hustling, whether it was walking the trade show with a handful of business cards or chasing important buyers down the aisles or making deals for television coverage (yes, frogs can get you some interesting perks). During many of our trade shows, we would have neighboring vendor's praise us for all of the visitors and attention we would get at our booth. In reality, we went and got them.

In trade shows, as in business, people rarely come to you. You need to go to them and give them reason to come to you.

Entrepreneurship is not for shy people. The same energy and enthusiasm you display to your employees is the same needed to attract clients, investors, cajole vendors, settle disputes with customers, and so on. Successful businesses are often associated with the entrepreneurs who start them, and often those entrepreneurs are outgoing role models for others. It is not necessary to run a business, but it most certainly helps.

INTERNET AND SOCIAL MEDIA

As we started distributing to Brookstone and hundreds of other small retail stores around the US, we were still strapped for cash. As much as we wanted to hire a public relations firm -- and we had more than a few courting us -- it just was not in the numbers. Our budget and all of our focus was on directing Wild Creations through its incredible growth spurt.

The great thing was due to our growth, and because we were both constantly promoting the company, we garnered a great deal of publicity organically. We also never shied away from when free publicity came to us.

During this time, we learned quickly the power of social media for increasing visibility and generating organic buzz. This was really emphasized in the fall of 2010, when we had the opportunity to have the EcoAquarium featured on the *Today* show on NBC. The segment was titled "Hot Toys for the Holiday Season," and Al Roker was to moderate the discussion.

Thinking we were going to get a massive boost in attention by having our frogs lauded on television by Al Roker, we called our website hosting partner and asked for more bandwidth and scheduled a few extra people to handle the flood of orders we were expecting.

The segment aired, and while we did have a few additional hits on the website, hardly any visitors converted to sales. We also did not see a significant impact in phone calls. It was rather disappointing to be sure.

Just about a week later, we had our EcoAquarium reviewed by the "mommy blog," Pioneer Woman. Its author, Ree Drummond (who later had her own show on The Food Network), wrote a shining review of the product and provided a link to our website and a discount coupon code for her readers to order online. At the time, she was one of the largest mommy bloggers online, with well over a million subscribers. That endorsement gave us a tremendous bump in web traffic, and the link and coupon code turned out to be a huge success, generating many times the number of sales as those generated by Al Roker.

The impact of social media and the power of peer reviews did not go unnoticed. We shifted our marketing tactics away from "old" media, such as radio and television, and quickly adopted new channels to reach customers, such as Facebook, Twitter, blogging, and other social media sites. At the time, social networking was a relatively new and inexpensive way to raise visibility and gain traction in the industry. We continued to promote the frogs and our new products through specialty retailers and ASTRA, but we felt like we had found a new and untapped resource.

By now, we all know the power and benefits of social media. Believing that it is the magic solution for a business's growth, however, is not realistic. In order for social media to really have an impact, you need a strategy that includes regularly generating useful, relevant and entertaining content and, more important, engaging with you customers. When you execute a great strategy, it turns your content into a tool for converting sales, and it turns your readers into promoters as they share and talk about your brand.

Pete: During those early days, Rhett and I both spent countless hours experimenting with social media. We would watch how our fans were consuming posts and content, which led to more shares. It was difficult to measure the impact on the business, in terms of conversions or revenue, but because we were small enough at the time, it was easy to see when posts were picked up and correlate them with a measurable goal.

Quite honestly, I think it's imperative that every company have a social media strategy. As it is more adopted by companies and customers alike, the importance will not necessarily be in how it impacts your business in a positive way but rather how much NOT having a strategy could hurt your business.

Rhett: In business and especially as an entrepreneur where your name is behind everything, you have to get right up into people's faces and say, "Here I am, here's what I can do, and this is why you should know me." You have to be the one who stands out in the crowd. When you can't be in someone's face, social media can do the job for you.

EXPANDING TO NEW MARKETS

One of the most valuable skills an entrepreneur can act on is finding opportunities to grow the business in new markets. This includes identifying new ways to use your existing products (line extensions) and developing new products that compliment your brand (brand extensions).

It is also important to have a sharp focus on the markets you target. For example, if you have been selling scrapbooking kits, and you develop a new tool for changing the crankshaft in a 1983 Buick, you're probably not going to find success with your existing network of customers. On the other hand, if you have developed a patented new scrapbooking glue or a proprietary technology to enhance the experience, you are much more likely to leverage your existing client base to not only buy your extensions but to also attract new clients.

In order to stay ahead of trends and changes in your industry, it is crucial to keep your finger on its pulse at all times. The best way to keep up with your industry is to simply read and stay informed. You can do this by regularly reading industry magazines, following pertinent websites and blogs, subscribing to industry social media feeds, or simply getting customer feedback. Some of your best ideas will very likely come from having your "ear to the ground" and reacting quickly to how consumers are using and feeling about your products.

All business expansions will most likely need funding of some sort in order to properly plan, develop and execute. In fact, a good rule of thumb is to treat new market expansions and product development as if they were brand new start-ups, because in many ways they are.

MANAGING VERSUS BUILDING

As we have pointed out in our previous chapters, we spent much of our time in the early days managing the day-to-day operations and sales of the company, which ultimately left us very little time to work on building the business. We were driving, visiting clients and customers, raising money, and going to trade shows, all of which almost led us to miss our grand opportunity at the New York Toy Fair.

We were working in our business rather than on our business.

It is a very troublesome trap that many entrepreneurs fall into. For the well being of the entrepreneur as well as the organization, however, you need to find a balance between the daily business grind and the more important business building efforts.

Every company needs both managers and builders (among many roles). These require two completely different skill sets, and a skilled manager may never become a skilled business builder, and vice versa. As an entrepreneur, however, especially in the start-up phase, you have to do both. Managing the business can be addictive and often serves as your comfort zone, but it should not become a distraction from the actions needed to grow it.

To evolve into the entrepreneur who can handle both aspects, here are a few helpful tips.

1. **Find the right team**. Surround yourself with talented people (arguably more talented than you in certain aspect of the business) to whom you can delegate the responsibility and authority to make important business decisions.

2. **Create a culture of collaboration.** In addition to having people on your team who you can trust, you need to create the culture in which they can thrive. As long as all of the individuals are willing and able to work effectively in teams, you will get much more benefit to encouraging collaboration among your staff.

3. **Develop a feedback loop.** Much like collaboration encourages teams to find the best ideas through iteration, having a feedback loop that encourages a constant flow of constructive feedback ensures that you move beyond poor business decisions and avoid making the same mistakes again.

COMPETING WITH THE BIG GUYS (AND GALS)

When growing your company, it can get increasingly more

intimidating as you face off with larger (and some case, much larger) competitors. The important thing for entrepreneurs to keep in mind is that every big company was once a startup themselves and probably considered the underdog at one time. The truth is that while larger companies have more resources, smaller companies have much more flexibility. This agility is what allows new entrepreneurs to find, maneuver and exploit opportunities -- as long as the business is properly prepared to do so.

Look for the gaps

Big competitors often have big gaps in their product offerings. Be careful here, as starting a company to take advantage of these gaps can put you at the mercy of your competitor if they adapt their product in order to take away this differentiation.

Give your customers solutions

Focus on the needs of your customers, and specifically those ailments that are not being satisfied by existing products and services.

Find a connection

People want to buy from other people, not companies. The more your customer feels connected to you the better they feel about doing business with you. Social media has made it incredibly easy to quickly engage with your customers and create that connection.

Be original

In addition to being more agile in their strategy, smaller businesses have much more flexibility to be creative and innovative in the way they develop their brand. At the end of the day, however, you still need to execute your strategy and deliver your value.

Be honest

Transparency is critical in today's market. The ease at which customers can find and share information puts the power of message directly in their hands and has created incredibly savvy consumers. For this reason, if you attempt to hide or manipulate your message, they will know and, more important, be willing to call you out for it. Encourage honesty and diplomacy throughout your organization.

GOOD TIMES

Executing a well planned out growth strategy pays great dividends, both financially as well as mentally. We got our big break with Brookstone, and although the logistics were a huge challenge, we made it work. During our big break out years, we sold tens of thousands of units across Brookstone as well as our special retailer partners. Word of our success began to spread throughout the toy industry, which led to numerous residual references.

Brookstone did very well with the frogs, which they called the "Frog-O-Sphere," even featuring it in the window of their Times Square store. It eventually went on to become their second best-selling overall product in 2009 (behind the remote control helicopters, which were all the rage at that time). More than units sold and revenue generated, the relationship with Brookstone proved we had the ability to scale and serve larger retailers, which proved to be more valuable.

Wild Creations went on to receive numerous toy industry awards and be recognized as an Inc 500 company not once but twice. In 2010, we were recognized by the South Carolina Chamber of Commerce as the state's fastest growing company. The runner up company, a Charleston-based government contractor called Pegasus Steel, produced steel reinforcements for all U.S. military vehicles. This fact led one news outlet reporting on the award to frame the recognition in a unique way.

"This all begs the question: What is stronger than steel? Apparently frogs."

We could not have framed that any better.

CHAPTER SEVEN

Chase the vision, not the money;
the money will end up following you.

-- Tony Hsieh, Founder and CEO, Zappos

FINANCING YOUR BUSINESS

If working for someone else can be likened to swimming laps in a heated pool, entrepreneurship can be compared to swimming against the current in cold surf.

Trying to run a startup business without adequate funding, however, is like swimming in a riptide, in cold surf, with burlap bags full of obese garden gnomes tied to your ankles. Oh, and did we mention the sharks?

Though you often hear of businesses that started on shoestring budgets or with a few personal credit cards and eventually became Fortune 500 companies, the truth is that the vast majority of entrepreneurs fail, and they fail because of one thing: they run out of money.

Unless you are already independently wealthy with resources to start a business (kudos to you), more than likely you will need to find money to start your business. Financing is one of the most important and challenging aspects of your business. Take out too much money, and you will be at the mercy of your lender. Take out too little, and you will run out. Take out the wrong kind, and you may severely handicap your business.

DO THE MATH

For starters, entrepreneurs should not attempt to guess at their financial needs. Even if you are not an accountant or financially inclined, you should be able to sit with a piece of paper (or a computer and spreadsheet) and create estimates for your inventory, office expenses, equipment, vehicles, fuel, mileage, utilities, warehouse space, employee wages, taxes, travel, etc. If you need help, a simple Internet search can yield any number of samples and templates. Better yet, start with a current IRS Schedule C form, which itemizes tax-deductible expenses your business might encounter.

Once you have an idea of what you need, be prepared to add at least 20 percent as your contingency.

BANKS

By the time we finished our due diligence as part of our acquisition of Wild Creations in March of 2007, we had come to the conclusion that the cost of the business was more than we wanted to spend. We were sure, however, it was under-valued, and we knew how to capitalize on it. Given the fact that we were buying a company with existing revenue, we decided to secure a bank loan for what we estimated would be necessary to provide us a runway to get fully operational

When we applied for bank financing for Wild Creations, the housing market was at a frenzy height, and banks were looking for anybody with a good credit score. Ours just happened to be stellar, which helped us secure an early business loan with absolutely no previous entrepreneurial experience.

It was a magical time.

These days, bank financing is as difficult to find as a unicorn. Entrepreneurs must present a very sound business plan and show collateral (house, car, classic Hot Wheels collection, or that original #1 Spider Man comic book). The collateral must be valued the same or more than the amount you are attempting to borrow, and you must demonstrate a risk-free way to pay back the loan regardless of how your business fares.

And, all banks require a personal guarantee on loans.

In other words, as one banking friend told us shortly after the financial crash, “Banks will only lend to businesses that do not need it.”

In reality, banks were right to crack down on their lending practices, because unless you do have a means to pay the loan back, a bank loan is one of the most inflexibly tools you can find for a new business endeavor. Regular monthly payments and strict terms make this instrument especially restricting on a business with little early cash flow. They may also restrict how you apply the money in your business.

The upside to banks is that they do not want to own or manage your business, nor do they really want the assets you have provided as collateral. Banks want regular monthly payments, with interest, so they can eventually package your loan and sell it. That’s banking.

In some cases, a business loan may be your only option. Just be certain to read the fine print and understand what the bank expects.

A quick word about Small Business Administration (SBA) loans, which are bank loans that are guaranteed by the U.S. government and, hence, much more attractive to banks.

The SBA loan application is extensive and intrusive, but if you meet the criteria, it can be a great way to help a new startup get funded. Just keep in mind that banks are still administering the loan, and therefore you will still be bound by the strict terms and covenants of your agreement.

INVESTORS

Investors are typically people or organizations that have piles of money to invest in small and large businesses with the hopes of allowing their money to make even more money. Every investor is different, starting with the stage of a business at which they provide capital.

Angel investors, invest at the very early stage of the company, typically in the startup stage. They can invest funds as early as your idea and as late as an expansion. Angel investors are typically your family members and close friends, but as you grow and gain leverage, you may find larger funds or wealthier individuals willing to invest in your idea. Just keep in mind that with the tremendous amount of risk involved with these early stage investments, investors expect to be compensated well for taking on that risk.

Venture capital investors, typically a firm with collective funds from many wealthy individuals, also invest in early stage companies, but typically after they have developed working models and have some proof of concept.

Private equity investors, also typically a firm with collective funds, invest in established companies that are staging for growth. PE investors often invest millions to tens of millions of dollars and seek companies with strong cash flows against which to leverage the company's fast growth plans.

In all cases, entrepreneurs need at least a basic business plan and a well-developed pitch. The nice thing about investors is that they will be much more flexible with how you apply the funds and, to a great extent, how you pay it back. Investors want all funds applied to the business and the business growth plans -- not servicing debt. Therefore, most investment terms are not based on payback schedules but rather equity schedules.

Every investor may have different ambitions and expectations, so it is incredibly important to understand how to negotiate an amenable agreement for all parties. You also need to understand the role of the investor in your company.

Active investors want to be involved in the operations and management of your business, in addition to owning a stake in your company. They may bring in their own people if they are not convinced the current team is effective.

Passive investors are silent partners who want no active role in the business. As long as you are making money for them, they will stay out of your hair.

Investors essentially become partners in your business, so do your research, find the proper counsel and advisors, and set the right expectations.

After Wild Creations' big break, we put together a very aggressive business plan to take the company to the next level and become a real force in the toy industry. To do so, we needed money -- and a lot of it -- so we developed a very detailed plan and started pitching to any investor who would listen to us.

We first looked at other companies in our industry and how they raised capital. We compared the five top companies we admired and looked for similarities in their fund-raising procedures. We left no stone unturned, interviewing consultants, brokers, attorneys, accountants, and people we viewed as mentors to help us in our search.

We continued to run into the conundrum that Wild Creations was too large for venture capital but too small for private equity. More important, so many investors had just gotten burned by the global financial crash that many were pulling their money to the sidelines and waiting out the storm.

Like the unfortunately timing of our start, it turned out that the timing was just wrong when we started searching.

INVESTOR CATEGORIES

Based on our extensive research and relationship building during our fundraising, we lumped potential investors into three types:

1. **The numbers investors:** These are the guys who think about *numbers, numbers, numbers*. These investors are concerned mainly with the bottom line -- how will they get their money back? Will it be from sales of shares, sale of the company, or percentage of the profits? They will pore over profit and loss reports, analyzing every revenue stream and every expense. They love charts and graphs and spreadsheets and will constantly be checking up on you to see how the numbers are looking.

2. **The "Let's make a deal!" investor:** This type is a wheeler-dealer gets excitement from the making of the deal itself. These people are high rollers, often willing to take more risks than the numbers investors. They're less concerned with day-to-day operations, and more concerned with return on their investments. They care less about the specific of the business, as long as it has a good chance of being successful.

3. **The investor with a heart:** This investor is often interested in causes and making a positive impact in the world through investing in companies with a cause. Your business vision

should line up with this investor's ideals. For example, if your potential investor wants to contribute a portion of his earnings to protect free-range prairie chickens, and your business involves fried chicken and/or taxidermy; you might not be a good fit. If you have a product that helps to mitigate flood damage and this investor is concerned with protecting people in Bangladesh from monsoon rains, you might be the perfect match for this investor.

SELLING YOUR IDEA

Regardless of what type of investor you are courting, your business plan needs to satisfy the three C's for investors -- it has to be **compelling, complete, and convincing.**

1. **Compelling.** Your product or service has to be innovative, unique, and exciting in its potential for profitability and furthering the interests of the potential investor. It has to have a "wow-factor". With Wild Creations, we felt it definitely satisfied these criteria -- a desktop aquarium that doesn't need cleaning, is environmentally sound and educational, and has two cute little frogs? Wow.

2. **Complete.** While business plans are organic and always changing, you need to demonstrate that you have thought out the details necessary to make the business successful. The plan should answer *who, what, how, where, when, why, and how*, in the end explaining why your product or service is the greatest thing since ham-and-pineapple pizza and why you are the team to make it happen.

3. **Convincing.** To get investors to embrace your idea, it will require the best sales pitch you have ever made in your life. Regardless how great you believe your idea to be, if you do not radiate confidence and enthusiasm from every pore, you will have a tough time closing the deal.

Do not expect a lot of attention from investors who are not involved in your market. A room full of tech investors, for example, is not likely to be interested in your traditional cupcake bakery. Look for investors who have worked with other companies within your industry.

Once you have your plan, you need to work on what is know as an "elevator pitch," or a 30 to 60 second compelling description of business idea. The idea is that if you were to step into an elevator with an influential investor whom you have been trying to meet, you only have that time in the elevator with the investor to convince him or her to invest in your company.

Assume this time in the elevator is no more than sixty seconds, so that is all the time you have to make your pitch.

We do not recommend using the "STOP" button as the alarms will surely interrupt your pitch -- as will the police and fire departments.

For this elevator pitch, you have to be compelling but also concise. You cannot screw this up. Investors do not have time for people who are not prepared to quickly explain to them what they need to hear. For this reason, you should write and rehearse and rehearse again your elevator pitch until it is ingrained in your head.

DO YOUR MARKET RESEARCH

We have been shocked at how many people only do peripheral research on their potential markets, or none at all. Some entrepreneurs are simply overconfident in their idea while others just lack the initiative to research. Regardless, you cannot skimp in this area.

If you are unable to explain why your product or service will matter to you customers and how it is solving a problem that the market or your competitors is not already solving, your chances of getting financing -- or even the time of day -- from a potential investor are no better than a snowflake surviving on a hot plate.

You should understand and be able to clearly explain:

What is the market need? What problem is your product or service solving?

What is the market size?

Why are you better prepared to solve this problem than existing or new competitors?

How will you get your first customer? How will you get your 100,000th customer?

Is your exit strategy viable in your industry?

Lastly, when it comes to securing investor money, entrepreneurs need to get used to rejection. Remember, courting investors is like courting a sweetheart. You will do well to remember the old adage; "You have to kiss a lot of frogs before you find your handsome prince (or princess)." Maybe *one million frogs*.

Oh yes we did.

OTHER INVESTOR OPPORTUNITIES

It is important for entrepreneurs to not get caught up in the popularity of venture capital and angel investors. Yes, these are great avenues for smart and aggressive entrepreneurs, but an investor could possibly be a friend or relative who is willing and able to help. While tapping a friend or relative for help can be risky and make for some very uncomfortable family gatherings, it could also be the motivation you need to persevere through tough times.

Nonetheless, it will require no less of a sales job than you would use on more formal investors. It goes without saying there needs to be a high level of trust on both sides in this situation. Nothing throws a monkey wrench into personal relationships like money issues -- especially lost money.

Pete: Even with the bank loan and all of our savings in the business, we felt we needed more money to allow us the flexibility to do with Wild Creations what we felt would make it successful. That's when I called my dad, the man with the 800 credit score, and asked him to help. And he did. He mortgaged his house and became a silent investor.

We could have bootstrapped the business, but I was confident in our ability to make Wild Creations successful, so asking my dad for a "line of credit" was easy to do. As it turned out, when the financial markets collapsed in 2008, that additional capital is what saved the company from becoming illiquid.

Rhett: I put in all of our saving and took on a second mortgage to support my family as we got Wild Creations off the ground. Like Pete, I was confident we could make Wild Creations work, and in the end, I never second-guessed those decisions as what was needed to get the job done. In a way putting it all on the line is what motivated us to never give up. In my case I had to make it succeed because we had put everything we had into the business.

INVESTING IN YOURSELF

One characteristic, above all else, is key for entrepreneurial success: Having confidence in your abilities to succeed and investing in yourself and your business.

When the economy crashed in 2008, we were maxed out financially. We had run out of money, and credit was not only scarce but also being taken away. It was a desperate scramble for us to find cash and operating capital to keep the doors open.

This was when we started talking about cashing in our 401(k) accounts.

Working professionally in corporate America for years, the golden rule of retirement planning -- never to touch your 401(k) -- is beaten into our understanding of universal law.

As an entrepreneur running your own company, however, you should embrace the idea that your business is your retirement. Investing in Fortune 500 companies is a comfortable bet, but in the end, you have no control of the direction of the company. With your company, you are in complete control of your own destiny.

For us, we made the decision that we would rather our 401(k) investment be in a company we were in complete control over. So we decided to cash out our accounts to get us through this rough time.

We took a big hit with the fees and taxes, but we had enough money to push through that second summer and make the business work. In truth, we had no other choice. It was either close Wild Creations and preserve our meager retirement fund or gamble it all on ourselves.

> **Rhett:** Credit is important for a business, but you should not rely on it to manage your business. It can quickly dry up or be taken away entirely. It's that simple. It may sound clichéd, but we also learned everything is a balancing act and you learn how to juggle priorities. You have to look at what you can get done today versus what you can put off until next week. You prioritize and go from there.

We were content with the financing decision we made for Wild Creations, and it while we were never able to secure investor capital, all turned out well in the end.

Of course, that was until we were faced with our biggest business challenge, one that could potentially close Wild Creations.

Cue ominous music ...

CHAPTER EIGHT

It's hard to beat a person who never gives up.

-- Babe Ruth, Hall of Fame Baseball Player,
New York Yankees

AND ALONG CAME PETA

Wild Creations was growing at an exciting and frantic pace. We were managing the growth as well as possible, and, for the most part, had tackled and overcome all of the challenges we had faced, from flooded neighbors to employee beat downs to extortion.

One thorn that continued to cause us issues was PETA. As mentioned in a previous chapter about employees, we were growing so fast we were forced to hire people off of the street to keep up with production. One guy, who we will call Kevin, was working out wonderfully. He was a fantastic salesman, worked well in the warehouse, and just seemed to be an all-around great guy.

One day in November of 2009, he did not show up for work. He called and indicated his mother in Florida was sick, and he needed to attend to her.

Completely reasonable.

Two weeks later, an "undercover" PETA video surfaced online purporting to show Wild Creations mistreating the frogs we handled. At the time, we were just gearing up with Brookstone to sell a private-label frog aquarium, called the Frog-O-Sphere, for their holiday season. We had leveraged heavily to service Brookstone and its 300 stores for the upcoming Christmas season. We were already running into issues with managing orders -- we were still printing and hand sorting orders, sometimes three or four thousand at a time -- so we were already stumbling to keep them happy.

PETA sent the video link in a massive attack campaign that delivered tens of thousands of form emails to Brookstone's CEO. The email demanded Brookstone discontinue selling Frog-O-Sphere else feel the wrath of PETA's membership.

Interestingly, the video, even in its doctored form, never showed anything horribly controversial. We did, in fact, handle the frogs in a professional manner, and it was clear many of the "questionable" scenes were staged or edited. Almost all of them involved Kevin doing something in the warehouse, so it is easy to conclude he was responsible for most of the purported injustices. To add a dramatic effect, he had distorted his voice to have a low and ominous tone. It was convincing, but very easy to discredit.

Regardless, when the CEO of Brookstone contacted us about the incident, it was a shock. This was a public company, with investors, lots of them, most of whom were conservative money people who avoided conflicts that could affect the stock price. If we lost the account with the impending holiday season around the corner, it would most certainly mean doom for Wild Creations.

We scrambled.

> **Rhett:** The video actually showed Pete talking to a couple of people at a trade show, explaining how to sell the aquariums. Kevin edited the video and framed the scene as Pete being insensitive and uncaring about dead frogs, caring instead only about sales and profit. What Kevin conveniently left out is the fact that Pete was talking with members of a charity we

> supported. We had donated every aquarium during the trade show to their charity, Amazonas, which raises money to fund a medicine boat that traveled up and down the Amazon to provide absent and much needed medical care to children. Clearly, that was not a profit-making trade show for us.

We always figured we would be targeted by PETA, and indeed our problems with them started many months before. PETA began working with freelance writers for small local newspapers up and down the east coast, often slandering Wild Creations for its animal rights abuses. Because these articles were often riddled with lies -- they often reported our warehouse in North Carolina -- we never really took them seriously.

Even before the undercover video came out publicly, the county police arrived at our warehouse to investigate a complaint of animal abuse they received from someone identifying themselves as PETA. When they arrived, we were very open and transparent and allowed them to freely walk through and check out the entire operation. After the inspection, the officers actually laughed at the complaint, acknowledging that out of all of the places PETA complained about, our warehouse should have been the least of their worries. The authorities later released a public statement absolving Wild Creations from all of the complaints.

Of course, PETA never published any retractions rebutting the misinformation they had published or that Wild Creations was cleared of any wrongdoing. More disappointing is the fact PETA never called us directly to talk to us about our product, operation, or handling practices. Up until that time we were able to work with and eventually satisfy every animal welfare group that contact us with concern.

All of them except PETA.

The most disturbing part about our problems with PETA was not the betrayed trust of the undercover video. It was not the multiple times we had to deal with police about complaints. It was how they treated our retail partners. Instead of contacting us to discuss their concerns, PETA would take to social media and email campaigns to inundate our retail partners with hate messages and misinformation. Sometimes, they would even organize protests outside of retail stores that carried the EcoAquarium.

This was upsetting because many of our clients were small retailers, "mom and pop" operations, that were already struggling to compete with large box stores and online retailers. They did not need, nor did they deserve, the overly aggressive bully tactics PETA employed.

For us, we were prepared from the onset of this new campaign. For example, we were very careful to make sure our handling practices were best in the industry. We had endorsements from veterinarians and even a herpetologist. We had documentation and even our own research on frog handling. We even had some of our packaging and shipping practices adopted by FedEx. All of this was readily available to anyone who requested it.

The vast majority of the stores we worked with understood and resented the methods employed by PETA and kept the product. Unfortunately, even with all of the material to support our product and discredit PETA, the pressure was too much for a small number of our smaller clients, and a handful dropped the product. Again, we were not necessarily upset about losing the account as much as bitter about the stress and anxiety they caused these small business owners.

ANY PRESS IS GOOD PRESS

As soon as the PETA flap started and the Brookstone CEO got involved, we went into crisis mode. Up to that time, the Frog-O-Sphere was the second bestselling product across all Brookstone stores behind the remote control helicopter, which was just hitting the market at the time. Customers loved the frogs, and

Brookstone loved the margin, so the CEO wanted to make this work while satiating his investors. Unfortunately, protests at Brookstone stores were being organized on social media, and he started to get cold feet about bad press.

We returned to our "war room" -- our small cramped shared office -- to strategize. For an entire weekend, we tuned everything out to focus on what we needed to do. We ended up crafting most of the public statement for Brookstone, working our information into press releases that supported the product. We communicated with Brookstone's legal counsel, managers, and on numerous occasions, directly with the CEO.

We knew we had a crisis, but we also knew we had to deal with it professionally and expeditiously. Brookstone dropping the product was not an option, as it certainly meant the closing of Wild Creations.

> **Pete:** I was impressed with how our war room efforts went down. In addition to fielding concerns and complaints aimed at Brookstone, we had people calling us and complaining. Most were people who had never owned or used the product and simply had questions. Unlike those who called and screamed angrily and were unwilling to listen, we were empathetic and diplomatic with these questions. We carefully worded our responses, and I believe our approach actually took many people by surprise.
>
> We shifted attention from the reports about animal abuse to the fact that PETA's agenda basically calls for abolishment of all pet ownership, which we simply disagreed with. When we explained PETA's motives, most callers empathized with us.
>
> For Brookstone, we drafted a response along these lines, saying essentially there was enough evidence to support the benefits of the product and the proper handling practices of Wild Creations, so the company would continue to carry the

product. The CEO seemed content, but he was still worried about the organized PETA protests of Brookstone.

DEALING WITH BULLIES

There is a scene in the classic comedy, *You've Got Mail,* where Tom Hanks quotes a line from *The Godfather*, telling his email pal, Meg Ryan, that in order to save her little bookstore from a fierce big-box competitor, she must "go to the mattresses." Meaning, of course, she must fight back against those who are out to do her and her company harm. This mentality to fight and protect your business is spot on, especially in the face of someone seeking to undermine and ultimately threaten you and your company.

PETA employs bully tactics to further their agenda, and like all bullies, they want the fight and the attention. Moreover, PETA is a large bully, with over three million members, three hundred employees, and over 34 million dollars in yearly revenue. So how do you combat a large and imposing bully who is calling you out to the playground to lay a beat down on you?

If you fight out of pride, you might cause a few bruises, but ultimately you just give the bully the attention he wants, which inevitably encourages and invites him back for more. Instead, you take the high road and ignore the bully until they find another person to annoy.

When we dealt with PETA, we never resorted to the same name-calling or mudslinging or misinformation campaigns. We simply put the facts out there and let our customers and the public decide. To do anything less than being completely above-board and objective will create weaknesses that your antagonist will exploit. Look no further than political campaigns of the last two hundred years or so.

Rhett: In some respects, we did not need to discredit PETA. Many of their own campaigns did this for us. Their organization was on the fringe, prioritizing causes such as breast milk for ice cream instead of fighting puppy farms. You have to question an organization that promotes its own porn site and at the same time euthanizes thousands of pets in its own shelter. It was clear, sadly, that they sought headlines more than impact.

We believe in continuous improvement and would have worked with anyone if they could help us be better -- but we were not going to be bullied.

Pete: One of my proudest accomplishments with Wild Creations is how we handled and overcame the challenges of PETA. We were prepared, diligent, transparent, and above all fair. We never took the situation lightly, and we never stooped to that level of intimidation. We fought and persevered through doing the right thing.

Rhett: You cannot let others define your business. Business owners are going to have issues that tax them, whether it is a competitor down the street, a special interest group like PETA, or some other challenge. If you have the respect and trust of your customers, you can muster through almost anything together. You have to fight for your product and what you stand for. You cannot always go toe-to-toe with them, but you can certainly out play them.

THE PROTEST FIZZLES

As the rumored PETA protests at Brookstone stores approached, we were regularly on the phone with the Brookstone CEO to hammer home our message of not backing down. PETA utilized social media and their membership to capture the attention of news stations, which were ready to cover the protests. PETA focused on a New York Brookstone store, which they assumed would bring more people and attention. We continued to assure them that the protests would be more bark than bite, and Brookstone stayed strong.

The truth is we were not completely sure about what would happen.

The day of the scheduled protest came. Several news stations double-parked media vans outside the Brookstone near Times Square.

We waited for news.

As the reports came in, we were told two people showed up at the store. One person held a sign reading, *"Don't Sell Frogs,"* while the other individual, dressed in a six-foot tall frog costume, danced outside. It was a complete misfire on PETA's part. Moreover, the two news broadcasts about the event interviewed patrons who had purchased the Frog-O-Sphere and were touting what a great product it was. It was fantastic press for Brookstone and Wild Creations.

Over the years, we had numerous other "threats" of protests, especially against our larger stores and chains. In every case, nothing happened. In 2010, we were finalist of the Ernst and Young Entrepreneur of the Year. Prior to the formal event, the organizer called to inform us they had received notice of a PETA protest organizing for the event and we would have two plain-clothes police officers hanging in the wings to protect us.

While we were flattered they would go to this level of protection, we tried to assure them that, based on our experiences with PETA, nothing would materialize, but they insisted. On the evening of event, true to form, absolutely nothing happened.

We did, however, make a couple of new police officer friends.

THE REAL CRISIS

With the PETA threat seemingly diffused and Brookstone content, we started feeling confident that the holiday season was going to be a homerun. We leveraged up more on Brookstone, putting a full time delivery team in the northeast to hand delivering EcoAquariums to the busiest stores, assuring the would never be out of stock. We had everything riding on Brookstone that holiday season.

Pete: One a Friday evening in early December, I was at a Christmas party with my wife when I received a text from Rhett: "War Room 911." This was serious.

We connected by phone, and he informed me the Center for Disease Control (CDC) had issued a public statement linking a nationwide salmonella outbreak to the particular type of frog we sold. The report was being covered by every major news agency, and while they did not mention Wild Creations by name, they used an image of the frog from our website.

Most alarming, it was children who were getting sick. We had discussed and even tried to strategize every bad case scenario we could come up with, and by and far, sick kids was the worst. I turned to my wife, kissed her, and told her not to expect me home.

Rhett: Within thirty minutes, we were both back in our "War Room," and for the next 48 straight hours over the weekend, we researched the issue, called and emailed anyone connected with the report, drafted PR statements, talked with our partners, and fielded calls from customers.

Our office and warehouse were typically closed on the weekend, but no phone call that weekend went unanswered and every email had a response within an hour. For obvious reasons, Brookstone was at the forefront of our concern. We had not heard from them, but we were certain we would soon.

> Again, the idea of failing or not bouncing back from this was never considered.

In hindsight, the earlier experience with PETA helped us tremendously. Without a doubt, the CDC salmonella report was a much more threatening issue than store protests by a radical special interest group, but the "practice" of dealing with PETA helped us handle the CDC issue calmly and timely.

By Sunday night, we were able to isolate the problem and determine that our frogs were not responsible for the outbreak. We updated our website, issued press releases, and even changed our outgoing message by adding an extension for inquiries.

We were well ahead and prepared to handle business when the office opened on Monday.

By the time the rest of the staff arrived that morning, we were able to debrief them before most of them were aware there was even an issue. As well, we called the Brookstone CEO early that morning to inform him of the issue. He was already aware of it, but was happy we had called him and already taken the initiative to resolve the issue.

By midweek, we had diffused the problem completely. Our effort to create and promote a public awareness campaign about the problem was eventually lauded by the CDC, who used Wild Creations as an example for other animal suppliers.

PETA persisted, however, even after we were able to discredit their claims, after Brookstone and the vast majority of our customers continued to carry the EcoAquarium, after fighting back all of the bully campaigns, and even after we were able to diffuse the CDC issue. They continued to linger in the shadows, issuing occasional press releases and continuing to push email and social media campaigns against stores. Their campaigns now leveraged the CDC report with the undercover video, untruthfully and dishonestly linking us to the problem. Time and time again, we were prepared and always able to overcome their harassment.

Interestingly, PETA came remarkably close to closing down Wild Creations early on, but it turned out we owed them thanks for helping us become better crisis managers.

SNEAKY PETA

PETA was relentless and strategic. They focused their attacks during our busiest and most important times of the year, including Easter, when we would ramp up for the summer, and Thanksgiving, when stores stocked up for the holiday.

After a couple of years of trying unsuccessfully to undermine Wild Creations, however, we believe it became clear to PETA that they were not going to stop the sale of our frog EcoAquarium, so they instead turned their attention and tactics toward our frog supplier.

Up until this time, we had a single supplier for our frogs, a faulty strategy for any business, especially when our company depends almost completely on frogs. Our supplier, however, had been in the business of breeding frogs and other aquatic animals for over forty years, and even at the height of our growth, when we were shipping over ten thousand frogs every week, he never once had an issue meeting our demand. As well, he was a straightforward, no-nonsense guy who lived a very simple life, and after meeting him in person, you got the sense that if there was every going to be a problem, we would know in plenty of time.

We did have back up suppliers, two of them in fact, but because of the dramatic price advantage we had for the volumes we ordered, we never needed to use them.

In April 2011, a few weeks before Easter and as stores were stocking up, our frog supplier phoned to inform us that our next order would be the last for a week. Typically, we ordered every day, as we rarely kept frogs in our facility for too long. After digging, he indicated that the local health department had been putting a great deal of pressure on him about the salmonella issue, and even after his tests of our frogs continued to yield negative results, he decided to close his facility and allow investigators on premise to review his handling practices and conduct more tests.

His closing was, in his words, "to get these assholes" off his back.

> **Pete:** I supported his cooperation and completely understood where he was coming from, but I was very concerned given the critical time of the year leading up to Easter. I called our primary backup supplier to place an order, and she indicated she had heard that our primary supplier was shut down -- because it was the same supplier she used. I phoned our second backup, a much smaller operation, and he indicated he purchased frogs from our primary backup. It turned out that our main frog guy supplied most, if not all, of the African dwarf frogs in North America.
>
> Even though our backup suppliers had secondary sources, they were extremely limited and much more expensive, and priority was given to their best customers. We were screwed for sure, but we figured we could gut it out for a week.
>
> One week passed. Then a second week passed. Then a third.

During this time, the local health department's tests were all returning negative for any contamination. After every test, however, the inspectors would require another test, then another, then another. We started calling the local health department ourselves to assist and put pressure on them to allow our supplier to ship the uncontaminated frogs. They refused and continued their investigation.

Four weeks passed. Then five weeks. Then six.

We were bleeding money carrying significant overhead with no frog revenue. We had also just opened an office in Oakland, California, in anticipation of a container of an entire new product line on the water from China. Leading up to the inspections, we had a comfortable cash position, but after a few weeks with significant cash outflow and inventory deposits due, it became apparent we needed to take evasive action.

Even with our remarkable growth and relatively strong cash position, banks still would not even consider us as a client. Sitting on the sidelines, licking their wounds from the housing market bust, banks made lines of credit impossible to get -- except for the companies who clearly did not need them. We were also pursuing an aggressive investor search to seek capital, but as we explained, that search turned up empty.

Toward the end of local health department's investigation, the CDC made a public announcement identifying the frogs in the salmonella breakout as being from our supplier. The announcement, however, went further issuing a warning that essentially said while selling and owning African dwarf frogs was not illegal, any company or individual buying them should not buy from this supplier.

This was unprecedented: a federal agency proclaiming publicly that a company should be boycotted, even though they were doing nothing illegally and, in fact, continued to test negative for any contamination.

> **Rhett**: In our minds, the CDC announcement is what solidified this as a PETA attack. The timing of the health department's investigation and the unprecedented slander of an innocent, private company by the CDC, all had the familiar scent of a PETA campaign.
>
> After the CDC announcement, we took it up a notch, contacting local and state legislators and lobbying them to close the investigation. Once influencers at the state level got involved, they were shocked to discover that, despite our

> supplier continuing to test negative for any contamination, the local health department continued to hold up shipments and was hurting innocent people.

Seven weeks bled into eight, until legislators finally got involved, and the local health department issued a decree that our frog supplier could finally ship again. Interestingly, the CDC never accepted the local health findings and continued to publicly and shamefully call for a boycott of our suppliers frogs.

By the time our supplier was able to ship, the damage had been done. Over the next several months and through the end of 2011, with our reserves all but depleted, we ended up rescinding much of the new inventory we had purchased and closed our California office almost as quickly as we opened it.

The most heartbreaking outcome was the fact we were forced to terminate almost 40 people from our Myrtle Beach warehouse, including an amazing team of six mentally handicapped employees who excitedly worked four days a week, as well as one young and wildly ambitious military veteran who managed our Oakland warehouse. Unlike the hiring follies we experienced at the start of the business, we had managed to piece together a fantastic, hard working, and loyal team. We often had cookouts on Fridays, and the staff had monthly "pot luck" lunches to celebrate everyone's birthday that month. This team was solid. They were close. And, while it probably was not a surprise for most who watched the investigation of our frog supplier unfold, it was no less difficult and gut wrenching to give them all the news.

> **Rhett**: We survived the long saga with PETA, the local health department, and the CDC, but not unscathed. I suppose this was what PETA had wanted all along. Unfortunately, they continually fail to see the collateral damage they cause along the way. In addition to the hard-working and innocent people who were let go, there are the countless stores they harassed and bullied. I can understand if Wild Creations or its products

were actually harming animals, or if people were really getting sick, but time and time again we discredited those claims.

More important, we never ran from the accusations. Instead of being part of the problem, we chose to be part of the solution, doing everything in our power to make the public aware of potential issues, pursuing and absorbing the cost of working with industry professionals to make certain our handling practices were top notch, and so on.

None of this is what PETA wanted. Headlines, money, and memberships are their only agenda.

Pete: For obvious reasons, we are avid supporters of animal welfare organizations, including PETA for the most part. The disappointing thing about PETA is that there are so many worthy welfare causes to pursue, like puppy mills, overcrowded poultry farms, or inhumane slaughterhouses. Instead, we see PETA targeting small companies with bully-like tactics just to get a few small victories at the cost of innocent, hardworking families. Worse, they prioritize projects like "Sexiest Vegetarian of the Month" instead of turning focus to their own animal shelters, where thousands of animals are euthanized every year. Why? Headlines.

In less than a year, we went from the award-winning darling toy company of the century to a company hanging on by the skin of their teeth, about to go belly-up. The fact that we stayed in business is amazing. We did eventually persevere and make it work, but we emerged as a completely different company.

Every struggle and failure is a learning experience, which is why no entrepreneur should ever regret a decision, a fight, or an outcome.

MANAGING SPECIAL INTEREST GROUPS

Here are a few takeaways and tips for dealing with special interest groups:

1. **Be Prepared**. Understand the potential threat of special interest groups that could find your company and products to be offensive and ripe for an attack. Do your research and don't dismiss any as nonsense or unrealistic.

2. **Choose Your Battles**. Most hostile special interest groups just want attention. They will employ bully tactics to undermine your company, often attacking your customers, as well as you. Like most bullies, engaging with them will just stoke the fire, but ignoring them can deflate their enthusiasm and encourage them to pursue another fight where they can garner more attention. If the group is not hurting your business, do not engage (but be prepared).

3. **Be Transparent**. If you are forced to respond, be honest about your business and products. Don't hide anything, lie, or embellish unnecessarily, as this will just raise suspicion and eventually hurt your credibility. You will sound more credible if you have and stick to factual evidence and use endorsements to back you up.

4. **Take the High Road**. While hostile groups will engage in false statements, slander, name calling, and embellishments, do not return the sentiment. Providing your customers and the public with a professional response with an "agree to disagree" approach will make the other group appear adolescent in their tactics and discredit their claims.

5. **Don't Back Down**. When it becomes clear that the hostile special interest group has no interest in cooperating, do not give in, regardless of the intensity of the attacks. Encourage your customers and vendors not to succumb

to the pressure as well. Bending to the group, especially when you have done nothing wrong, will only provide fodder and strength for future campaigns.

6. **Do the Right Thing**. Ultimately, most special interest groups (even PETA) have a good cause. If you actually find the concerns of the group are valid, then work with them to improve your business and products. This can lead to a great relationship and, possibly, an endorsement. Just don't count on that from PETA.

CHAPTER NINE

Every worthwhile accomplishment, big or little,
has its stages of drudgery and triumph:
a beginning, a struggle and a victory.

-- Mahatma Gandhi, Political and Spiritual Leader, India

HAVE AN EXIT STRATEGY

We have talked about sticking it out through thick and thin -- doing what you have to do to keep your doors open and cash flowing. We've offered ideas about how to overcome a good number of the adversities you might face in your business, as well as examples of what to do and what not to do. What we haven't really discussed yet is an exit strategy.

Big dreams aside, the fact is most small business owners have no exit strategy for their businesses. Business owners focus on growth and survival and often not on an exit or succession plan for when it is time to get out.

This is important, because planning your exit starts the day you open your business. How you set it up, how you run it, the people you put in place, all of the initial setup, planning and execution affects how you eventually get out of the business.

And if you believe you will not get out of the business, keep in mind that unexpected life events happen. You get married or divorced, you have children, you or a relative gets sick, or you simply just burn out. These are things that you cannot plan for -- but you can plan ahead for making an exit easier.

Your exit strategy will in large part depend on the type of business you have and what you want it to do for you. Here are five basic exit strategies based on the type of business you run.

1. **Lifestyle company:** In this scenario, you have built the company into something small but efficient, and just want to hand off the management and operations to someone else. You keep it small and make enough for a comfortable living. This is a good strategy for a small business you have run for years and can now use to fund that motorhome you intend to cover with decals from every state you visit.

2. **Selling to a friendly buyer:** In this case, you sell the business to a customer, a family member, a longtime vendor, or a faithful employee. You can do this through an owner-financed deal, where you carry the note and let your buyer make installments payments (not recommended except in situations involving absolute trust), or your buyer finds the necessary financing and purchases the business from you outright.

3. **Acquisition:** This is probably the most common exit strategy. You sell your business to another business. This can involve a complete transfer of all assets or a controlling portion. Choose the former if you just want to cash out and be done with it and the latter if you still want to be involved in some way. Remember in Chapter Five where we discussed courting investors? There are many ways to structure such a deal, and it is best to employ accounting and legal assistance to better navigate your options

4. **Initial Public Offering (IPO):** This is where you sell raise capital through public markets in exchange for small ownership portions, or shares, of your business. This is less

common, very expensive, and is best reserved for larger companies with a considerable amount of future growth. It is also extremely complicated, and requires a team of financial and legal consultants to assure compliance with the mountains of rules and regulations pertaining to IPOs.

Unless you're a Wall Street genius or have one on staff, leave this one alone.

5. **Liquidation:** No one who starts a company is planning to liquidate it someday, but it happens more often than not. Most businesses fail within the first few years and are faced with dissolution in some form or another. In choosing liquidation, you simply call it quits, close the doors, and sell off the assets and inventory for whatever you can get, often to cut your losses. Generally, this is not the prettiest option, but if you can at least break even, you can walk away from it with peace of mind and no creditors hounding you.

   It's best to choose this option to keep from going completely belly-up before your debts become insurmountable and you have to file bankruptcy, which will haunt you for up to ten years. If you seem to be careening toward this end, be sure you find that balance point where you can liquidate and still be solvent. Don't wait until it's too late, or bankruptcy may be your only option.

MAKING THE DECISION TO EXIT

In the beginning, we had no idea we would be in the situation we found ourselves. Remember, our original goal was to create and manage a holdings company that would eventually compete with the likes of Berkshire Hathaway, where we wheeled and dealed and pulled the strings that made the money flow.

We never dreamed we'd be making our living selling little frog habitats.

We still had dreams of growing the business and diversifying our product portfolio, and we still had a solid reputation in our industry. We clearly needed money, however, to achieve this with Wild Creations, and because of our situation, money became even more difficult to secure.

We were passionate, experienced, and had a clear path to take Wild Creations to the next level. We just needed investors to achieve our goals.

For months, we pitched our 600-page business plan relentlessly to investors, until we finally met a group of investors interested in our plans. After months of negotiations, it became clear that we needed them much more than they needed us, which clearly moved the pendulum of leverage in their favor. Although our team was what made Wild Creations successful, we eventually agreed to relinquish controlling interest in our business in order to raise the necessary capital.

In our mind, it was much better to own a small part of something big then a large part of something small.

Our original meeting with our new partners was in September 2011, and we closed the deal in February 2013.

> **Rhett:** Pete and I realized we needed capital to get to the next level, instead of just doing the same thing we'd been doing over and over. We knew we needed an investor, which meant giving up a part of the company to get the money. We needed cash and credit to grow. We looked everywhere -- every bank, every investment firm, and under every rock. We hired a consultant to help us find money and to properly structure ourselves to come across as professional as possible. It was time to 'grow up' and make another move. We did the whole

dog and pony show with investors and even had people fly in on their personal planes to check out the business. The process of finding investors took us over two years.

Pete: Suffice it to say, after the debacle of 2011, we hunkered down and got back to basics in 2012, focusing on the frog business. We kept operating as a frog business while negotiated the acquisition throughout the year. Personally, for me, selling the business was a no-brainer. We were stuck, but we had these partners who believed in us, the product, and the company, so it all had to work out for the best.

HOW TO APPROACH SELLING

Making the decision to sell is not always an easy one. Maybe you want to retire. Maybe you want to cash out and spend the rest of your life working to save the rainforests. Maybe you're just burned out and want to tackle a new venture.

In our case, we exited in order to make our goals possible.

Regardless, when considering selling your company, consider these factors.

Are you willing to give up control? Whenever you decide to sell, you have two options. The first is to sell and get out of the business completely. The second is to sell part of your business to a partner or partners and actively staying part of the business.

If you decided to sell to a new partner, ego and emotion can get in the way. You are, after all allowing new people into the business you built with your own sweat and tears. It can also be risky, especially if the new owners want to take it in a different direction.

Of course, you will (or should) have done your due diligence long before selling, and you hopefully have found a partner with whom you are comfortable getting into business. But the lingering concern -- the elephant in the room -- always comes down to ownership and control.

In the game of business, there is only one golden rule -- he who has the gold rules. So if you are in the unfortunate position of seeking a partner that will help fund a business, which is what most of your investors are looking for, you will most likely be asked to relinquish control.

Of course all of this is negotiable, and ultimately a successful investment deal only works if both parties are satisfied with the final outcome. For entrepreneurs, however, it is important to ask yourself that tough question: how much is control of your company worth.

You need to ask yourself: do I want to own all of something small or part of something huge.

With our deal, we were happy to relinquish control but stay involved. It meant that we could get fired at any time (although we did negotiate employment agreements) or our partners could decide to take the business a different direction. In the end, however, we were both educated and experienced business professionals looking for a means to grow our business or exit, so deciding to sell was easy.

Your business plan is your most important asset. Since we had just endured the worst year ever, our only leverage was our business plan, the 600-page document we lugged around to countless meetings. The plan you use to sell your business is a lot like the plan you put together at the beginning to court investors, with the added details of what the business has accomplished to date and what the future plans are. If your ship is taking on water like ours was, you absolutely have to show them how it can be fixed.

Honesty is still the best policy. Investors will want to know the mistakes you have made and how you intend to fix them and mitigate them in the future. Never present your company as flawless and never fudge the details. They need to know everything about you, warts and all (pardon the frog pun). Your company history should be as accurate and honest as possible.

Also keep in mind that investors value entrepreneurs who have faults or who have failed or otherwise made bad decisions. They particularly value those that have learned from these faults and mistakes, as it demonstrates that you have already failed on someone else's dime and time.

Be aggressive in your pitch. This does not mean being adversarial, rather it means being proactive. Decide in advance how you will address the toughest questions investors will ask. Be enthusiastic about your vision for the company's future. If you don't show 100% confidence, they will eat you alive.

Negotiate every detail. Do not be afraid to ask for what you want, and know in advance what you are and are not willing to give up. Get everything in writing and be certain that all legal points are clarified. If you intend to stay employed in the company, make sure your responsibilities, privileges, and job security are spelled out in great detail. History is full of stories about supposedly savvy entrepreneurs who were booted out of their own operations on technicalities or vagaries in their contracts, with no legal recourse.

If this is your first sale, or if you have any doubts, find a mentor to advise you along the way, and never skimp on accounting and legal consultation.

NEVER LOOK BACK

As an entrepreneur, your business life is often riddled with *woulda-coulda-shoulda* scenarios, but you can't go back and undo previous decisions or circumstances. You can only move forward and learn from every experience.

Mistakes will happen, bad decision will be made, and opportunities will be lost, but in the end, if you are making decisions with your company values and all stakeholders in mind, there is very little you can or should regret.

CHAPTER TEN

If you're going through hell, keep going.

-- Winston Churchill, former Prime Minister, Great Britain

THE PERSONAL TOLL -- IS IT WORTH IT?

Running your own business is like walking a high wire without a net -- wearing clown shoes. It is dangerous and stressful. There will be more personal sacrifices then when you work for someone else. You have a higher stake in the company, and its failure means your failure.

Do you have what it takes to endure?

> **Pete:** The beginning stages of the company were tough for me. I really didn't anticipate how difficult it was going to be. Our first Christmas season, for instance, was an incredibly dark period for me. I'm a Christmas Eve baby, so Christmas and my birthday, "Petemas," has always been an important time of celebrating and spending time with family. I'm the type of person who listens to Christmas music in November -- it's that serious.
>
> During Wild Creation's first Christmas in 2007, however, we were struggling to make ends meet, and we had a number of mall kiosks around the southeast. Because we went through a series of poor hirings for the kiosks, Rhett and I were forced

to spend our Christmas standing at a mall kiosk-selling frogs. I remember Christmas Eve, my birthday, I was working a kiosk in Atlanta, Georgia. It was painfully slow, which in itself was distressing, and I stood there until the mall closed at 10:00 that evening. Afterwards, I drove to a sushi restaurant that happened to be open. I ate sushi and drank sake with the general manager of a Wal-Mart and the restaurant's staff. That was how I spent my birthday: no family, no celebration, no presents, just solitude.

It forever changed my emotions toward Christmas, and in particular the songs that I repeatedly heard in the mall that year.

Maybe the more difficult thing to accept was just two years earlier, I was in Central Asia doing business development with important and influential people, such as the president of Kazakhstan and Michael Porter of Harvard fame. That Christmas night, I was decked out in my "Froggy Style" long-sleeved Wild Creations shirt, eating a California roll and wearing the restaurant's celebratory birthday sombrero. I still have the Polaroid from that night to remind me of the feeling.

Later that evening, I drove six hours back to Myrtle Beach, which gave me a lot of time to think and reflect and doubt. I was broke and alone. I'd given up a lucrative job for a struggling frog business in a terrible recession. It was not part of my "plan."

After that first Christmas, I really felt the desire to punt and sell the business, but because I had borrowed most of the start-up capital from my father, who had mortgaged his house to help, there was no way of getting out without sacrificing his home. It was not a fun position to be in. I was always stressed and unhappy. I wasn't sleeping, and when I was, I wasn't sleeping well. I had a chronic case of bronchitis, which was clearly linked to my stress.

Rhett and I had a gut-check talk I still remember. It was on the back bumper of our delivery van, one afternoon shortly after Christmas. He was stressed, too, but made it clear he was not going to give up. His attitude was remarkable, considering the fact he had spent the entire Christmas on the road away from his very young children. He never talked or complained about it though. He just did it, with a quiet resolve.

His perseverance, along with a little pep talk, got me to give up the idea of finding a way out. It was still a bit stressful for a short time, but I eventually learned how to push through the stress.

Rhett: I was there, too. Working on Christmas Eve wasn't anything I'd ever done in any previous job I'd had. Ever. Like Pete, a couple of years earlier, I was working out trade deals between two different countries and interacting with high-level people. I was making important things happen. Then, just a short time later, I found myself at a mall selling frogs.

I remember one day that holiday when I ran into an old college classmate of mine while at the kiosk. He had become an attorney, and I remember when he saw me standing in front of the kiosk, wearing a shirt that read, "Froggy Style." The look on his face was plain and clear.

Wow... this guy has hit rock bottom.

Maybe I had. Pete's incentives for sticking with the business were different than mine. My wife was home with our kids, taking care of them. In my mind, I couldn't give up. I couldn't quit. I didn't have a Plan B at the time. In 2008, my wife said she would return to work in the Foreign Service. We delayed her job offer as long as we could, but we knew she had to go back. At some point, she had to do it because Pete and I weren't paying ourselves, and we needed a way to live. It wasn't turning out like it was supposed to, but her going back to work saved us from financial ruin. She eventually moved the family back to Washington, D.C. This sacrifice was the first major business decision that saved us.

Though my wife has been gracious through it all, it doesn't mean we didn't have those tough conversations. The expectation I'd given her when it first started was that our business was going to be textbook, a piece of cake. What do you say eighteen months later when you're still not paying yourself? It was a huge lifestyle adjustment. I liked being debt-free and having a good credit rating. Money matters are some of the worst stresses on anyone, and what was going on with the company was stressful.

FINANCIAL STRAIN

We have mentioned this before, but one of the biggest challenges to an entrepreneur will be when finances are stretched to the breaking point. When things go south, the first thing affected is your cash flow. Cash flow is the lifeblood of a business, and when that is cut off, you are in big trouble. The resulting chain reaction can be devastating to everyone involved in the business, including your family.

After our frog supplier shut down in 2011, we went several weeks with no frogs and, hence, no revenue. For most companies, this would have been death. Fortunately, we were coming off an incredible year and had reserves. When those started to dwindle, it was our strong relationships and the goodwill we had developed with our partners and stakeholders that kept the doors open. We made very difficult business decisions during that time, including being forced to cancel new business partnerships and cut several employees with whom we had close relationships.

Our goodwill came from our policy of honesty and constant communication. Our clients and vendors appreciated the fact that we kept them in the loop during this tough time, though it came at a price. As the situation progressed, many of our vendors got nervous and reduced our credit terms, in some cases rescinding them all together. Like the beginning of the business, we became a cash operator. While that may be seen as a reason for hiding things from our vendors, our struggles were not a secret. Most businesses these days cannot hide from trouble, so when stakeholders and partners get wind of it, it is much better if you deliver the news rather than hearing it second hand.

It may cause some uncomfortable conversations, but in the long run, your business will benefit.

MANAGING STRESS

Never convince yourself into thinking entrepreneurship is easy. For many, the anxiety and pressure can be overwhelming. Until you learn how to manage and control the anxiety, be ready for the gut wrenching and nauseating feeling you will get throughout the early stages.

For instance, when your phone rings on the weekend or after hours, it typically means trouble. You still need to answer the call and deal with the situation.

Those calls become much more stressful when you realize they may affect the lives of everyone around you.

After we surfaced from our frog supplier issue and business resumed normally -- as normally as it could -- we focused on paying back our vendors. We took some liberties with our larger vendors, focusing instead on our smaller vendors first, with whom a few thousand dollars meant the difference between making payroll and staying open. We also had to prioritize the vendors we needed to keep the businesses open, which meant pushing banks to the backburner. This hurt our credit, of course, but we kept the lines of communications open with everyone and were transparent about our strategy to get back on our feet.

That tumultuous time made our vendors, employees and customers very nervous. Some vendors never returned our credit, and banks turned a cold shoulder -- or colder shoulder, as the case was. All of this hampered our ability to ever fully return to the frog part of the business to the size we once were, though the experience made us much better entrepreneurs and enabled us to continue to piece the company back together.

FINDING BALANCE

The hardest part about entrepreneurship is balancing your business and family relationships. It is a given you are going to put forth far more than the typical forty hours per week and be apart from your spouse and family often, sometimes for weeks at a time.

Not all personal partners are amenable to this kind of schedule and financial stress. We have been very fortunate to have women in our lives who support our entrepreneurial "habit" and who have been supportive through our experiences with Wild Creations. You not only need to understand what you are getting into with running a business, but also make sure your family "stakeholders" understand. They need to be on board and share your vision.

Though many entrepreneurs enjoy successful marriages, there are a great number of horror stories that result from entrepreneurial endeavors. Many relationships do not hold up under the stress and strain of entrepreneurship. If you are married and considering entrepreneurship, make sure you and your spouse are aware of the schedule, financial commitment, and physical and emotional grind that will be involved.

It is almost impossible not to bring home the stress of a hard day or week in the trenches. Just as you strive to keep open communication with your business associates, you must commit to keeping honest, transparent, and open communication in your family. Life is not normal, by any measure, and to a certain extent, you can and should leverage the adventure of entrepreneurship in your relationship.

> **Rhett**: I was on the road so often at the beginning, I missed a number of milestones with my kids. My wife was amazing and supportive, but I understood I had to get home. When things settled down, and we figured out how to ship the product, I was home much more. The New York Toy Fair, which we attended each year, always fell on the week of Valentine's Day and my birthday. Instead of looking at it as being away for these important dates, my wife and I made weekends out of it in New York. It's all about how you look at the issue.

Balancing and maintaining family requires effort, maybe as much or more than the business itself does. You need to know how to read the signs of family issues as easily as you can read signs of business issues, and you must keep them separate as much as possible. If you just had a knockdown, drag-out debate with an overly aggressive animal activist who compares you to Hitler (that is probably not going to happen to you, but consider something comparable), you cannot bring that stress and anger home to the dinner table. It is a tough skill to master, but you need to learn to leave the office at the office.

This is especially true if you have children, since your kids are sponges who absorb moods as much as apple juice. Additionally, if you are constantly working, you miss many of the events that bond you together as a family. There is a balance you can achieve, between family milestones and your entrepreneurial commitments, but it requires a great deal of practice.

Just remember, like sorting and prioritizing tasks in your business, you must make certain to do the same with your family. Be sure you and your spouse are in agreement about those priorities, and when a disagreement exists, find compromise. Whatever you do, never overlook this communication, because just as important as vision and goals are for your business, so too are those priorities for your family.

MAINTAINING SANITY

Entrepreneurship will test you to your absolute limits, mentally, physically, and emotionally. Like a sport -- or more specifically, a long distance competitive race -- success depends greatly on your ability to prepare, train and condition. While it impossible to predict every possible problem, issue, or scenario you and your business will run across, you can train and be prepared. A significant part of this mental training is surrounding yourself with people who will understand, empathize, and support you, such as your family, business partner, friends, and so on.

> **Pete:** We never expected to come across most of the crazy things that happened in the course of building Wild Creations. I don't think it was possible to conceive of them beforehand. What I have learned, and what I admire in other entrepreneurs I meet, is the ability to prepare yourself for the unexpected.
>
> I remember when I had the mental collapse when we flooded our neighbor's warehouse in the first month of operations. I was a wreck. Fast forward a few years to when our company stood on the brink of collapse with PETA and supplier issue, all while my wife was giving birth to our daughter -- the years of experience and conditioning myself to stress made this impossibly stressful combination of events much easier to handle than flooding an office. In fact, I recall that period of time being very happy, with a beautiful new baby girl to divert my energy.
>
> More important, I had matured as an entrepreneur, and I felt very confident we were going to pull through. Even if we didn't, I knew we would survive and live to fight another day. It's an

amazing feeling, but one you don't get sitting on the sidelines watching. You only learn this through experience.

In terms of where we are compared to where we started, there is no doubt we matured and emerged as completely different people -- better in many ways. We have both learned to manage the anxiety with more confidence. We are battle-hardened in many ways, which makes us wiser and better equipped to handle new challenges and make smarter decisions. It is a profound realization and understanding that regardless of what happens, good entrepreneurs -- indeed good people -- will overcome and persevere, even when things look their bleakest.

It is also a profound realization and understanding that can only come from doing and experiencing and practicing.

This, if nothing else, is what we hope to convey with this book to other.

THE FUTURE LOOKS BRIGHT

The story of Wild Creations is not finished. In 2013, we divested our interest to an investment firm in order to restructure the company, raise new capital, and grow the company again. The truth is Wild Creations never fully recovered from the frog supplier issue, and although we managed to pull the company from the brink and right the ship, we were still saddled with debt and had a shadow lingering over the company. The strategy behind partnering with investors, we believe, will give the business the boost it needs.

We also introduced a new brand identity in 2014, after the new partnership was formalized. We have a number of new initiatives we are very excited about, including a unique open innovation platform that allows Wild Creations to meet with new and promising inventors.

Our frogs and EcoAquariums will continue to be the backbone of the business, although we hope to expand on the learning experience for our young consumers through products that offer educational benefits and encourage interaction with nature, something we have been passionate about from the beginning. From frogs to radio-controlled rattlesnakes to electronic puzzles and games, we hope to establish the business as a leader in toy innovation.

FINAL WORD

Rhett: In one way, I wouldn't change what we went through or go back and do it another way. When you look back at what you've done as an entrepreneur, do you really want to start over and go through everything again? The answer is yes I would. I'm a pretty hard-headed guy, so I don't think there are a lot of things I'd do differently.

However, if I could go back, there would be areas where I wouldn't be so aggressive. There are mistakes or experiments I wouldn't advocate as much. At the same time, it's all part of the growing process. One of the reasons we grew so aggressively was because we took chances. You have to spend money to make money, right? You have to take risks. You have to be willing to work harder than you thought possible. You have to have discipline and drive. Those aren't just words, I believe they are essential for success.

Rocky Balboa nails it when talking to his son about life in the last Rocky movie, "It ain't about how hard you hit. It's about how hard you can get hit and keep moving forward. How much you can take and keep moving forward. That's how winning is done. Now, if you know what you're worth, then go out and get what you're worth. But ya gotta be willing to take the hits, and not pointing fingers saying you ain't where you wanna be because of him, or her, or anybody!"

The last 7 years, I learned I could take a few punches and still get back up. I learned that anything is possible. I learned that no is not in my vocabulary. I learned that success is not easy. I learned the value of partnership.

Pete: Looking back on the experience with Wild Creations, there is nothing I would change or do differently. Even with failures and the "dark times" I experienced at the beginning, with the non-stop anxiety, panic attacks and chronic bronchitis, the journey that brought me to today has made me a better entrepreneur and, to a greater extent, a better person.

I often compare the experience with having your heart broken. I would argue if you have never had your heartbroken, you really wouldn't appreciate love when it presents itself. The same goes with entrepreneurship. All of the lessons I learned, good, bad, and ugly, I would never have experienced if I hadn't tried and taken the risks we took. If I had never followed the entrepreneurial ambitions, and taken other risks along the way, the regret of what might have been would have been greater than any regrets I have now.

More importantly, I learned that as an entrepreneur, it is in nobody's best interest if you fail. For that reason, any major problem or challenge can always be worked out with healthy helping of communication sprinkled with moderate amount of diplomacy. In the end, there is no problem you can't negotiate and recover from. Once you realize that, there really is nothing to hold you back from pursuing your entrepreneurial dreams.

BIOGRAPHIES

Peter Gasca is from Phoenix, Arizona, where he attended Arizona State University and earned a degree in Construction Project Management. After spending half a decade in real estate development and homebuilding, he moved to Washington, D.C., where he received his MBA from Georgetown University, with an emphasis in Finance and Strategy. He then moved to Central Asia as a volunteer with Pyxera Global (formerly the MBA Enterprise Corps), and ended up staying to work as a business development consultant for USAID before moving to South Carolina to pursue his entrepreneurial dreams with Wild Creations. He currently serves as an advisor for Startup.SC and as an Executive in Residence at Coastal Carolina University. Peter and his wife, Flyura, have two children, Christopher and Amina, and live in Myrtle Beach, South Carolina.

Rhett Power is from Charleston, South Carolina, where he attended the Citadel and University of South Carolina. After an early career in politics, radio and public relations, he sold all of his worldly possessions and joined the United States Peace Corps, shipping off to Uzbekistan in Central Asia. Following the Peace Corps where he taught business and current affairs at Bukhara State University, he stayed in the region and worked with USAID as a business development consultant before returning to his home state to start Wild Creations. Currently Rhett writes for *Inc.* and *Success Magazine* on management, leadership and entrepreneurship. He just finished a second book on entrepreneurship which will be published by McGraw Hill in early 2017 . Rhett and his wife, Julia, a U.S. diplomat, have two boys Max and William, and for the moment live in Washington D.C.

INDEX

www.ingramcontent.com/pod-product-compliance
Ingram Content Group UK Ltd.
Pitfield, Milton Keynes, MK11 3LW, UK
UKHW020133250726
13967UKWH00002B/626

9 781634 139076